# THE FATHER BAKER CODE

*John Koerner*

As always,
Dedicated to the memory of
Anthony P. Losi
and
Salvatore L. Losi

Address all inquires to:
Western New York Wares, Inc.
P.O. Box 733
Ellicott Station
Buffalo, NY 14205
(716) 832-6088

This book was published and printed in Buffalo, NY

ISBN: 978-1-879201-61-3

*Cover bust of Father Baker was created by
and is used by permission of Susan Nowak.
susannowak@live.com*

*Back cover image courtesy
of author's personal collection.*

**Visit our Internet Site at
www.Buffalobooks.com**

# TABLE OF CONTENTS

# ACKNOWLEDGEMENTS

I would like to extend my deepest gratitude to the following people. Your individual contributions have been both large and small, but never forgotten, and always essential. You have been an inspiration to me, and have made this book possible.

Tim Ellis, Elizabeth Ellis, "Anne," Elsie Hertz, Norman Hertz, Nelson Smoczynski and his family, Carol Shoff, Mike Osborne and Rick James' Dealer, the staff at "C 2," Michael Gauchat, SFO, Joseph Metz, Daniel Metz, Brian Meyer, Joseph Ebert, Rob Lockhart, Barbara Lawrence, Vincent Barnes, Benedict Koerner, MaryAnn Koerner, Mary Losi, Mason Winfield, John F. Welch, Sue Nowak, Marie Sommer, Mary Lou O'Connor, William O'Connor, Grant Koerner, Sister Eileen Pinkel, Deborah Hatten, Dave Hatten, Father Robert McNamara, Marilyn Sheriff, Cristina Higgins, Patrick Higgins, Dixie Bryant, Stuart Sullivan, Danielle Buchbinder, Eric Buchbinder, Father Paul Burkard, Maureen Kanaley, Warren Baltes, James Koerner, and especially to my wife, Tammy, who helped to shape this book in so many subtle and creative ways.

# INTRODUCTION

Code. Few words conjure up such a depth of meaning, and even controversy, as this one. It implies a use of symbols to represent something secret or hidden, or perhaps a way of life, rigidly maintained by a select few. There is yet another connotation to this enigmatic word, a more classical usage that is less frequently employed in the United States than it is in European and Eastern culture. A code is also a rule, or even a set of rules that are systematically arranged.[1] Rules are essential in most human endeavors. There is the Military Code of Conduct, the Code Napoleon, the Socratic Code and many others, but one code that is lacking is in the area of the miraculous. Can we find a rule to explain why a human being is able to perform a miracle, even after death?

This is in part what we seek to do here. We will endeavor to explain that concept of "code" in different ways. The strange mix of suffering and piety that leads to the miraculous will be our code, or rule, to follow with Father Nelson Baker. This will lead us through our fresh discussion of his life and miracles. In Part One "A Saintly Life," we will delve deeper into his well-known life story, providing insight that no biography of him has yet offered, including new information on the silent suffering he likely endured nearly every day of his priesthood.

In Part Two, "The Lost Miracles," we will add to the historical record new mysteries that have come to light since the publication of *The Mysteries of Father Baker* in 2005. These alleged miracles show that people continue to pray to Baker, and apparently are still meeting with success.

This section will provide some of the latest information that has come to my attention, as yet unpublished, but keep in mind that I make no pretense to say that this is the definitive update on the Nelson Baker story. I am convinced that there are countless other stories out there that are being kept private. I have encountered some individuals who believe that such events are personal matters between themselves and God. They respectfully seek no notoriety. But others have come forward, some anonymously, to aid in our understanding of the ongoing story of this miraculous man. Through their stories we can marvel, and we can wonder. We are forever in their debt.

In Part Three, "Secrets of the Gauchat/Metz Relics," we will examine again the concept of code. As we noted above, a code can be a way of life rigidly maintained by a select few. There is no better way to describe the knighthood-like passion with which followers of Father Baker protect his artifacts, as we will explore in this section.

Finally, Part Four, "Unlocking the Vatican," will explain the canonization process, Baker's progress to achieve sainthood, as well the advantages and disadvantages unique to his specific case. It is now outdated to believe that logic, evidence, and reasoning are the enemies of religion. Instead, code-like rules and science can often help us to understand faith. We will see for example in this section how the Catholic Church has embraced science, using it to prove miracles beyond any human doubt.

Also, a brief word on term usage. Numerous times in the text we will encounter various relics of Father Baker. In fact, they are at the heart of many stories that lie ahead. Therefore, it is appropriate to define this term at the outset and explain how the Church makes distinctions among these sacred artifacts.

According to the *Catholic Encyclopedic Dictionary*, relics are the remains of venerated men and women, "either their entire physical bodies, portions of their bodies, or articles of clothing they used during their lifetime."[2] The Church allows for veneration of relics because it could lead others to emulate the pious lives of these men and women. Countless miracles have been recognized by the Vatican as having been worked through the use of a relic.

Relics are typically categorized into three classes. First-class relics are body parts of the venerated person, second-class relics are possessions (or pieces of possessions) of the venerated person, and third-class relics are items that are touched to the tomb or dead body of the man or woman in question. When we encounter a first-class relic in the text, it will be followed by this designation to properly identify it: "1CR." A second-class relic will be dubbed "2CR," and of course a third-class relic will have the label "3CR."

These markers will hopefully give us some context with which to examine this aspect of the miraculous. As we will see, relics are often used as a means of invoking divine power. However, with these classifications, one may be predisposed to assume that second and third-class relics might be less "powerful" than those favored first-classers. Yet, just like on an airplane, be wary of pre-judging someone simply based on where they are sitting. I only ask readers to approach this with an open mind.

Let us then begin again our quest to understand this enigmatic man, perhaps the greatest human being that Western New Yorker has ever seen. As historian David McCullough is fond of saying when speaking of the Founding Fathers such as John Adams, "we can never know enough about him."

*– John Koerner*

*Father Baker circa 1910.*

# PART ONE:
# A SAINTLY LIFE

*Chapter One:*
# A NEW PERSPECTIVE

"I'm going to send you to Father Baker's" was at one time the most effective parenting tool in Western New York. As the years stretch from the date of his death, many Western New Yorkers seem to remember less about Nelson Baker the man, but still seem to recall Nelson Baker as a threat.

One Buffalonian confided to me a terrifying story that happened to her in her childhood in the 1950s, well after Baker had passed. This particular girl's parents made a habit of threatening to send her and her siblings to Father Baker's on several occasions. On one particular afternoon, there was a knock at the front door. She peaked outside and saw two nuns dressed in their intimidating pre-Vatican II armor. The clothing that Catholic nuns wore in those days could often make even the most strident miscreant cower before their authority. This little girl was convinced that the game was up. Checkmate. Their parents had finally made good on the warnings. They were about to be taken away to Father Baker's. Rather than accept their fate, she and her siblings hid for hours, trying to avoid the inevitable. Eventually they were discovered in a closet, scared to death. No doubt it took a little convincing that the good sisters were only there collecting for charity.

The ironic thing about these idle threats that many parents resorted to was that Nelson Baker and his institutions were anything but the houses of horror that many children must have assumed they were. Baker was a Renaissance Man of boundless goodness, impeccable intelligence, stunning business acumen, and masterful creativity. He could speak, read, and write fluently in

Latin, German, Spanish, and English. He was an actor, a singer, an athlete, and a virtuosic musician, much to the delight of the boys who called him "Father" in every sense of that sacred word. It seemed that during his life, and even after his death, there was nothing he could not do, except perhaps walk on water - although we're still waiting for a story on that one.

The complexity of his personality is evident in the variety of photographs that were taken of him during various times in his life. Local artist and sculptor Sue Nowak has noticed this and has spent years studying Nelson Baker's face to create a bust of the OLV pastor. She has remarked how unusually different his face looks photo to photo, age to age, and therefore how difficult it was to make a single bust of him that envelopes the intricacies of his face and personality. Baker can be seen grinning, posing, occasionally smiling, often serious and even stoically unreachable in the images that survive. Worry, stress, confidence, and kindness seem to emanate from his eyes as they stare out from the past - his past.

Nowak offered the following comments on what inspired her to create the sculpture that graces the cover of this book.

*Having grown up in Lackawanna, I had heard of Father Baker most of my life. I had moved away for a number of years when I finished college. When I came back I realized how lucky we are to have a church like Our Lady of Victory here. Talking to people about the church made me curious about the priest who had it built. The more I looked into Father Baker the more I admired what a great man he was.*

*When I decided to create a sculpture of Father Baker, I knew it would be a challenge because of the limited number of photos of him. When I create sculptures of living people, I have them model for the sculpture and I also take photos at various angles as an added reference. With Father Baker, I found the photos challenging because in each image of him he looks like a different person.*

*There is always a challenge to create a three dimensional sculpture out of two-dimensional images. The photos show him at different ages and the angles of his head and face are different in every image. The qualities of the photos from that time are not as good as are possible today. Many photos are not in sharp focus. It is like trying to piece his image together from a puzzle. I started a bust of him as a young man, then decided that more people would probably relate to him as an older man. So the final bust of him is around 60-70 years old.*[3]

*Photo courtesy of Sue Nowak*

*Sue Nowak's Baker bust at an earlier stage of production.*

The Baker bust seems a fusion of his life experiences, as if the decades of pain, piety, and power are etched into the essence of the sculpture. That life began in Buffalo on the corner of Oak and Huron on February 16, 1841, or perhaps 1842. Before being ordained a priest at the age of 35, he lived an early life not unlike countless other sainted men and women throughout history.

St. Francis, St. Augustine, and St. Ignatius of Loyola are just three examples of men who did not enter a religious, God-centered life, until well into their adulthood. Each man, like Baker, spent much of their youth in the secular world. For many years Nelson Baker built a successful feed and grain business in Buffalo with his business partner, Joseph Meyer.

It was not until Baker reached the age of 28 that something changed in him. The summer of 1869 was a watershed season for this future humanitarian. He decided to leave his business, friends, and family to take a mysterious, private, trip around the Great Lakes to reflect on his life. Using his own savings, he visited shrines, attended Mass, wrote in his journal, and reflected deeply on his life. Quite often the question is asked, "When did Baker perform his first miracle?" Although we cannot answer this question definitively, this pilgrimage around the lakes is certainly the point in this young man's life when he realized that he was capable of something much greater. He returned home and announced to his family that he was going to be a priest.

However, the road to ordination would not be an easy one. On September 2, 1869, Baker joined the ranks of students (most of them a decade younger) at Our Lady of the Angels Seminary, the site of today's Niagara University. He would not be ordained until 1876. The intervening years for Baker were marked with an intense battle with a crippling skin disease known as erysipelas. In the age before antibiotics, this disease killed nearly everyone in its path. Baker suffered with a full share of lesions and sores all over his body. Not expected to live, he was given the Last Rites, the Catholic sacrament reserved for those on the very brink of death. Baker attributed his unlikely survival to God Himself, something he would be reminded of constantly by the limp he carried for the rest of his life.

Erysipelas also left this young seminarian with yet another legacy, a portal to the miraculous. When looking at Nelson Baker's reputation for performing miracles, one might naturally wonder how this man, or any other human being, could attain supernatural power. In looking at the past there are many other holy men and women throughout history said to be able to perform stunning miraculous deeds, all of whom had an intense piety. Yet there have been countless other holy people throughout history with an intense piety who have been unable to harness this miraculous power. Take for example your local parish priest. So what is it then that sets apart people like Nelson Baker and moves them into the category of wonder worker?

I believe that in Baker's case it had everything to do with his personal, physical suffering. Piety combined with suffering seems to lead to a profound spiritual empathy. St. Bernadette of Lourdes, St. Sebastian, and Padre Pio, are just a few examples of pious saints who suffered greatly during their earthly lives, and who in turn had strong reputations for the miraculous, both before and after their deaths. To put it simply, perhaps one must first know what it means to suffer and be healed in order to heal another human being. Saint Paul said it best in his second letter to the Corinthians.

> *Therefore that I might not become too elated, a thorn in the flesh was given to me, an angel of Satan, to beat me, to keep me from being too elated. Three times I begged the Lord about this, that it might leave me, but he said to me, "My grace is sufficient for you, for power is made perfect in weakness." I will rather boast most gladly of my weakness, in order that the power of Christ may dwell with me.*
> *(2 Corinthians: 12: 7b-9)[5]*

Yes, power seems to be made perfect in weakness, and erysipelas was not the end of Baker's weakness. Either in 1925, or 1927, Baker had one of his eyes removed after a difficult period of private anguish with a steadily worsening eye. This was when he was in his mid-eighties. Thus we have these two bookends on Baker's life, one with his skin, and one with his eye, that both caused him a great deal of misery. Is it just a coincidence then that there are such a large number of skin and eye-related miracles attributed to Father Baker, during his life and after his death?

Further evidence of the connection between suffering and the miraculous comes from a man whose life bears a striking similarity to Nelson Baker, none other than Pope John Paul II. Both men were actors, singers, musicians, war veterans, skillfully multilingual, and intensely devoted to the Blessed Virgin Mary. Both priests also endured their fair share of suffering. And yes, we can probably now say that both men were miracle workers as well. Just as in the case with Baker, the late pontiff has at least one miracle in his portfolio directly connected to his own suffering.

In March 2007, the allegedly miraculous healing of Sister Marie Simon-Pierre was brought to the attention of the Vatican's Congregation for the Causes of Saints. Sister Simon-Pierre claimed to have been completely healed of Parkinson's disease, the same ailment that Pope John Paul II suffered from and ultimately succumbed to.

On June 2, 2005, exactly two months after the death of the pontiff, the French nun informed her mother superior that she could no longer perform her duties at a maternity ward in southern France, due to her progressively worsening condition. That night, she and her fellow Sisters prayed solemnly and exclusively to the late pope to heal Sister Marie. When she woke up at 4:30 the following morning it was clear that something was quite different. "I bounded out of bed, and I felt completely transformed," she said. Sister Marie quickly told a fellow nun that "Pope John Paul has cured me." The Vatican is currently studying the case to see if it can be used to move the late pope closer to sainthood.[6]

Whether it is Parkinson's, erysipelas, eye problems, or a host of other human frailties visited upon history's mystics, the message is clear. Out of this misery can often come something greater, something so rare when genuine, and so little understood: the ability to heal another human being beyond all scientific understanding. This is the code that we seek to enter the miraculous. We will probe further into this matter in part two, "The Lost Miracles."

After Baker's long period of suffering as a seminarian, he was finally ordained on March 19, 1876, at St. Joseph's Cathedral in Buffalo, over seven years after he began his theological studies. He was promptly sent to St. Patrick's Parish at Limestone Hill, just outside of Buffalo. His assignment was to resuscitate the near moribund finances of the parish, and assist with the running of the institutions for orphaned boys. After four years as assistant pastor he was transferred to Corning, New York, at the age of 39. He stayed in Corning from January 1881 until approximately February 1882. There are at least five miracles associated with his brief stay in that southern

New York State town, which was then a part of the Buffalo Diocese.

However, that would not be the last time that Baker would hear from Corning, New York. Corning native and Rochester Catholic Diocesan Archivist Rev. Robert McNamara had a brief occasion to meet Father Baker in the early 1930s when the OLV pastor was approximately 90 years old. NcNamara never forgot this brief encounter. The two men discussed their memories and fondness for the quaint town, despite the fact that Baker's stint there was over half a century ago. McNamara noted that at first glance this old priest was nothing more than a frail man of average height, perhaps extending no more than five feet, five inches off the ground. Yet within that small frame he could not help but be struck by such an aura of strength, kindness, and mysticism that pervaded his entire being.[7]

After Baker's brief stint in Corning, he was transferred back to Limestone Hill, but this time as pastor. He would spend the rest of his life there, nearly half a century. During his second tour of duty at St. Patrick's, Baker restored the finances of the parish, changed its name to Our Lady of Victory Parish, added an infants' home, a nurses' home, Our Lady of Victory Hospital, a farm, and Our Lady of Victory Basilica. Baker oversaw the construction and funding of the basilica while in his mid-eighties. When it opened in 1925 it was completely paid for. In 1891, and then again 20 years later, Baker discovered and oversaw the construction of a gas well on the grounds of the parish. The continued operation (at least for the second well), existence, location, and depth of these wells all defied scientific understanding. Baker also provided for the education and training of thousands of children from around the world, and fed countless starving people throughout his lifetime.

Nelson Baker died on July 29, 1936, at Our Lady of Victory Hospital. After a funeral attended by at least half a million people, Father Baker was buried next to his parents in Holy Cross Cemetery in Lackawanna, within site of his beloved Basilica. Immediately there was talk of sainthood for this renowned humanitarian. By 1987, the Congregation for the Causes of the Saints named Baker a "Servant of God," essentially the first of three steps toward canonization, or "sainthood," something no American-born male has ever achieved.

Twelve years after Baker's elevation to "Servant of God" status, the Vatican advised Our Lady of Victory Parish to move the body of Father Baker inside the Basilica so that pilgrims could more easily pray to him, perhaps leading to the two required miracles to achieve sainthood, a process that we will detail later.

When Baker's body was exhumed, three vials of his blood were discovered that had been buried in a box atop his coffin. The blood had remained liquid for 63 years. Was this a miracle? The Vatican and Our Lady of Victory Parish each conducted independent tests on the blood. Both concluded that the blood's fluidity could not be explained by science, but more impressive was the fact that the blood was still active and not decomposed. It was behaving as if it was still inside Baker's body.

However, the Vatican could not accept this as a required miracle, probably for two reasons. First, the Church requires that all miracles must be 100 percent in nature. In other words, Baker's entire body would have had to have been preserved, or "incorrupt," not just the blood. Second, miracles of "incorruptibility," have been out of vogue with the Vatican since the 1980s. During that decade the Church allowed scientists to examine some of the so-called "incorruptibles," the group of holy men and women throughout history whose bodies have resisted various stages of decay. Much to the embarrassment of the Vatican, scientists found that many bodies had been stitched together, or had undergone embalming. Understandably, the Vatican has been hesitant to take chances with miracles of the same ilk.

Some might view this as a setback in Baker's canonization effort, but it should be viewed in context. The blood miracle is only one of many miraculous events attributed to Baker, and that is perhaps the strongest aspect to his cause. Many candidates on the road to sainthood reach a roadblock once achieving the "Servant of God" status because people simply lose interest, and few people continue to pray to these quickly forgotten souls. Without continued prayers and alleged intercessions, the Vatican cannot investigate and prove that a miracle took place. This is not the case with Nelson Baker. People continue to pray to him constantly, as will see in part two.

*Chapter Two:*

# BAKER'S SUPERHUMAN GIFT

As we tried to demonstrate earlier, there is an undeniable correlation between suffering and the ability to perform miracles. In Baker's life we can certainly point to his skin and eye ailments. But is there another, more mysterious and hidden side to this element of Baker's life? Such a question is at the heart of this book. We can only hope to truly know this man by continually trying to find out new things about him and look at old research in a new light. We can only know Baker the wonder-worker by going as far as we can into the mental and physical anguishes that he endured.

The thesis that Baker's skin and eye diseases provided a portal to the supernatural is credible enough, but I feel it may have one shortcoming. These events essentially bookended his priestly life, one as a seminarian, and one in his late eighties. What about the time in between, the intervening half a century, when he certainly was apparently at the height of his abilities as a miracle worker? What sustained him during this time, physically, spiritually, and supernaturally? How was he able to live in sound body and mind well into his nineties?

I would like to suggest that Nelson Baker may have possessed an ability that is found only among a handful of the most holy men and women in human history. This strange superhuman gift is called "inedia." It is defined as the "capacity to forgo food for months or even years without damage to the body or brain."[8] The 20th century Portuguese mystic Alexandra Da Costa lived on nothing but the Blessed Sacrament for forty days in the summer of 1943.[9] The nineteenth century German visionary Anne Catherine

Emmerich, also known as "The Seer of Dulmen," sustained herself on only water and the Eucharist for the last ten years of her life.[10] However, inedia has various levels of manifestation. Some thought to have this gift can survive on just the Eucharist as noted above, or even miniscule amounts of sustenance that normally would malnourish the human body and quickly lead to death.

*Baker in his 90s. (Left to right) Brother Stanislaus, Rt. Rev. Msgr. Henry B. Laudenbach, Baker, and Rt. Rev. Msgr. John C. Carr.*

Self sacrifice and suffering along with extreme piety yield miraculous results in this world and the next. Was inedia a part of this for Nelson Baker? Certainly we know that Baker led a life of self-denial. Very early on this trait showed itself in his personality. Late in 1869, while only a seminarian, Baker recorded in his journal an urgent plea. "With Thy help, O God, and the help of Thy intercession, O Holy Mary my Queen, I hope to receive sufficient grace, to avoid sin, and this most detestable vice of

Gluttony."[11]  On October 10, 1869, Baker set forth some parameters for himself. "Rules. God help me. Pray. I will eat no more Peaches. I will eat no more Pie. I will eat no more Custard. I will eat no more Bread pudding. I will eat no more Bread pudding sauce. I will eat no more Cakes. I will eat no more Tomatoes. I will eat no more Molasses."[12]

This type of discipline and lack of concern about the self, extended to other parts of his life. Rarely could anyone who knew Baker recall seeing him sleep, especially for extended periods, save for the times when he was found passed out from exhaustion after praying for hours at the altar. Nor would Baker seem to stop for meals. There was too much work to be done. In fact, near the end of his life, Baker remarked to his dear assistant, Brother Stanislaus, that he had not had the time to read a book for pleasure in over 20 years.[13]

Inedia is very difficult to prove because by its nature there would not be any specific stories to investigate, just a general impression of how Baker conducted his life. However, there is one inference that we can make with the help of modern science. Taking the earliest possible date of his birth, February 16, 1841, and the date of his death, July 29, 1936, we can plainly see that Nelson Baker lived just over 95 years. His impressive life span may be a clue to the presence of inedia.

For many decades, scientists have long suspected that something called "caloric restriction" may increase lifespan in various organisms such as mice. Caloric restriction is a fancy term for eating less. A lot less. Perhaps as much as a third of the calories that are thought to constitute a "normal" diet.

But what about people? Can the link be made in more advanced forms of life? In the September 21, 2007, edition of the scientific journal *Cell*, researchers from the Harvard and Cornell medical schools published their findings showing a link with humans. They discovered two genes that "act as gatekeepers for cellular longevity. When cells experience certain kinds of stress, such as caloric restriction, these genes rev up and protect cells from the diseases of aging."[14]

Perhaps now we can speculate on Baker based on this new information. Simply stated, if Father Baker spent vast portions of his life endowed with the gift of inedia, then he would have been a prime example of a person engaged in constant "caloric restriction." Also keep in mind that inedia is even more drastic than the one-third reduction used in the study above, with virtually no caloric intake among its mystical practitioners. Therefore, it seems possible to suggest that Baker's exceptional life span would have been a by-product of this, a by-product of inedia. Perhaps his 95 years are the best evidence we have for such a remarkable power.

Inedia seems to pervade his disciplined lifestyle, a grace no doubt he would have considered a gift to handle the enormous burden of his endless responsibilities. Logically, with food often so scarce at Limestone Hill, it would make sense that Baker would save every last scrap for his boys, and not for himself. Is it possible then, through his continued daily self-denials of food (whether self imposed or divinely assisted), that this provided him with a level of personal suffering that he could tap into when healing another anguishing human being? Was this Baker's way to sanctify himself, purifying his body to obtain the level of empathy I believe is necessary to reach the miraculous? Is this "piety + suffering = miracles" code yet again evident with Baker's suspected gift of inedia? We have previously noted Baker's power over nearly everything from Mother Nature to death itself. Did he have power over his own body? The question still haunts.

*Father Baker circa 1910.*

# PART TWO: THE LOST MIRACLES

# Chapter Three:
# THE COMA MIRACLE

In this section we will chronicle new miraculous tales attributed to the intercession of Father Nelson Baker that have come to light since the publication of *The Mysteries of Father Baker*. These are a testament to his enduring legacy, and to the faith of those who have suffered. We reserve judgment on these stories, merely reporting the basic facts as they were commended to me. I hold dear those who have honored me with their trust.

Our first story is of the anonymous kind, but it took place in this decade and was told to me directly by the father of the girl in question.[15] The details we can provide are concise but will serve to make a larger point.

The young woman involved in this alleged miracle sustained serious injuries as the result of a car accident. She was rushed to the Erie County Medical Center (ECMC) where she quickly lapsed into a coma. The physicians involved gave the girl very little chance of recovery, and forecasted at minimum an extensive comatose period, followed by mental and physical disabilities.

However, as is the rule in many Baker-related miracles, a relic of the late priest's was brought in to try to heal the girl. The relic used in this case though was not just any relic, it was the crucifix (2CR) that Baker himself had in his hands when he died. This same crucifix inexplicably cured a Lackawanna policeman in February 1938 who was told by physicians that he had just hours left to live. As we noted in *Mysteries*, that man survived another half century. With the girl at ECMC, the cross was brought over from Our Lady of Victory Parish and placed in her hands. According to her father, she "immediately" came out of the coma and began a quick and successful convalescence.

This seemed the perfect miracle to move Baker up the path to sainthood. Our Lady of Victory officials excitedly investigated the story and took the proper testimony to give to the Vatican. However, in the course of their digging, they came across one key fact that effectively put a metal rod in the spokes of their inquiry, and ended any hope of using the story as a required miracle. As luck would have it, a Jewish friend of the family heard of the critical condition of the girl and saw to it that a prayer was put in the Wailing Wall in Jerusalem, asking for her recovery. This theologically killed the investigation.

The Vatican requires that any miracle under consideration must come directly from the candidate in question. A family or an individual cannot pray to multiple sources, otherwise, theologically it is unclear who is responsible for the intercession. For example, if someone had cancer and prayed to Father Baker, and also to St. Jude, and then recovered, the miracle could not be used to help Father Baker achieve sainthood because the Church would say that is it unclear if Baker interceded, or if it was St. Jude who interceded.

This story thus serves to point out how difficult it is to get through the two miracle requirements for sainthood, a process we will explain in greater detail in chapter nineteen, "The Journey to Sainthood."

*Chapter Four:*
# THE SACRISTY MIRACLE

In the course of a lifetime it happens rarely. Maybe once. Meeting that person who strikes you immediately as having a special holiness, an inner peace that transcends explanation. The subject of our next story is just such a person. She has wished to remain anonymous. Of course we will respect her wishes, and thank her for the courage of sharing her remarkable story with us.[16] For our purposes we will call her "Anne."

This tale begins in July 1988 when this Buffalo woman was convinced that she saw a vision of Jesus Christ while she was praying. Her faith came alive again and she felt compelled to visit Medjugorje in August 1990. Since 1981, many have reported seeing visions of the Blessed Virgin Mary at this small town in Bosnia-Herzegovina in Eastern Europe.[17] Millions now follow the events there online, and read of messages allegedly given by Mary to a hopeful world, but often laced with many predictions.

However, the Church has never given an official backing to these reports. Among many Catholic faithful this does not matter, and they continue to believe in and follow the latest developments from this far corner of the world. I can still recall a visit made by Buffalo Diocesan officials to my Catholic grammar school, Sts. Peter and Paul, in the late 1980s. Our devoted, saintly, religion teacher, Sister Grace, had just returned from a visit to Medjugorje. Before the trip, she told our class how excited she was to go, and that she could not wait to share with us all that she would see and learn there. The day she returned however, she was told in no uncertain terms by the Buffalo Diocese that she could not speak a word about it to any of her religion classes. She obeyed the directive, but was visibly angry and crestfallen. To say the least then, Medjugorje is controversial, which, in part, helps to explain what happened next to Anne.

After her return from Europe, she began to speak of her faith in Medjugorje and her vision of Jesus. As an active member of a South Buffalo parish for over 25 years, she felt comfortable sharing feelings and beliefs to her fellow parishioners. The reaction was not what she expected. Many did not believe her and began to openly criticize her and gossip about her behind her back.

Anne was now faced with a crucial decision. Should she leave her beloved parish where she had served for over a quarter of a century? Could she find a new spiritual home that would welcome her? As many Catholics do who are confronted with a conundrum, Anne asked Jesus to bring a rose to her somehow as a sign that leaving the parish was the right thing to do. Sure enough she received a red rose within days and took this as a sign to put the pettiness and jealousy at that parish behind her. But where to go now? The large parish of Our Lady of Victory seemed the perfect safe haven.

Anne joined as a Eucharistic minister and served proudly at the parish for several years until in 1999 the unthinkable happened. The gossip, jealously, and persecution started again. People from her old parish started to spread false, destructive rumors about her at OLV. Seeking solace and guidance she went to the Father Baker museum in the basement of Our Lady of Victory Basilica in July 1999. In this section of OLV there are two authentic reconstructed rooms of Father Baker's living quarters, as well as several photographs and artifacts relating to his life and canonization process. Anne stopped at his mock bedroom and began to pray. She asked for Father Baker's help and guidance to see her through this difficult time in her life. Soon it was time to prepare for Mass so she headed upstairs to get dressed for the service.

Over the sink in the sacristy of Our Lady of Victory is an image of Father Baker. At that time, on either side of the portrait were two letters written in Latin. Both of these letters have since been moved to the Father Baker museum for public display. They are now both on the wall in the back

*The sacristy at Our Lady of Victory Basilica. The picture of Father Baker above the sink can be seen through the opening of the door.*

room in the museum, above a display case. This was done by the orders of the late Pastor Robert Wurtz.

The first is a 1926 letter from the Buffalo Diocese. At the bottom is a handwritten inscription that reads "certificate of consecration." The other is a 1924 letter from Rome that also has a handwritten inscription at the bottom. This one reads "changing title of St. Patrick's to Our Lady of Victory." Anne was reading this second letter when she began to feel "rays" coming into her heart from Baker's picture. The whole room then began to inexplicably fill up with the aromatic presence of incense. Moreover, this intense aroma seemed to be emanating from Baker's image. There was absolutely no incense burning in the church at the time. A witness to this was so scared and shocked that she promptly ran out of the room to bring in the priest. According to Anne, the priest and three other people confirmed the smell, and could not account for it. Anne took this as a sign of Father Baker's presence. She was convinced that Father Baker and God had heard her prayer and that they were with her to help her endure any further challenges at the parish.

However, this was apparently not the last she would hear (or more accurately smell) from Nelson Baker. One last beautiful gesture of encouragement was sent her way a few years later at an unexpected moment. One of Anne's most prized possessions is a Father Baker rosary made of crystal that she purchased in the Our Lady of Victory Basilica gift shop. In 2003, she was taking her rosary out of its case, and was immediately surrounded by the smell of a special flower. It was the same flower that brought her to Our Lady of Victory years earlier, and would now seem to confirm the wisdom of her decision. A rose.

*Chapter Five:*

# THE GHOSTLY MIRACLE

The following narrative is one of the most well-known stories in the folklore of Our Lady of Victory Basilica, mostly likely because it involved a beloved, long serving volunteer, Mary Timms. In fact, I would guess that there are several different versions of this extraordinary event that have been told, retold, and altered over the years. As with any piece of folklore, including this one, details change over time. Major points are sometimes forgotten, embellished, or even added. Such is human nature. However, at the root of many folkloric tales often lies a kernel of truth. And even more to our advantage, I was able to obtain two separate sources for this miraculous tale, both of whom received the story directly from Mary (who is now deceased). Rather than mesh the two sources together to form a single account, we will tell them independently of one another. In this fashion we can note the striking parallels between them, as well as the slight differences.

The first version comes from Elsie Hertz, of Hamburg, who was well-acquainted with Mary Timms.[18] According to Mrs. Hertz, Mary caught the attention of Father Baker when she was a young girl because of her name. Father Baker's love and devotion for the Blessed Virgin Mary is well documented. "My child, you will be blessed," the OLV pastor told her at their first meeting, most likely in the 1920s.

Later in her life, well after the late prelate had passed away, Mary fell gravely ill and was not expected to live. During the depths of her illness, Father Baker apparently appeared at the foot of her bed. She soon made a full recovery that she directly attributed to the man who told her decades ago that indeed she would be blessed. But this would not be the last time that she would see his apparition. The second time Baker came calling, Mary's life again hung in the balance, and this time without warning.

As part of her dedication to the Church, Ms. Timms was a long-serving member on the staff of the Our Lady of Victory gift shop. Part of her duties involved the occasionally lonely task of opening the store. On one particular day she was going downstairs to open the shop when she noticed a young man hiding under a cart near the entrance. She thought this was a bit odd, but proceeded to open the door anyway. The man immediately went inside, waited for her to get behind the counter, and then made, let's say, a bad choice. He jumped the counter and was now face to face with a terrified Mary Timms. He may have thought that this was the perfect crime. No security cameras. No witnesses. He was all alone with an elderly, helpless woman who was completely at his mercy. Or so he thought.

Before the man could fulfill his evil deed, much less even choke out a few words, a ghostly image materialized between himself and his intended victim. It was Father Baker, staring directly into his soul. The would-be thief turned "white as a sheet and ran out." There's no word if he raced upstairs to convert to Catholicism, but we're still checking on that one. When this dramatic event was over, Baker disappeared as quickly as he came, but Mary was convinced he appeared to protect her, and perhaps even save her life.

The second version of this story comes to us from Anne, the focus of the "Sacristy Miracle" chronicled above.[19] Anne received the story directly from Mary, having known her from their overlapping time serving at Our Lady of Victory. This second account has some striking details, and is much more dramatic than our first chronology. Here is that report as told to me by Anne.

Mary Timms headed downstairs to open the gift store and noticed that there was a young man, probably a teenager, crouching down under a cart near the door to the shop. After unlocking the door she went inside, and walked behind the counter. After a short period of time, the youth aggressively confronted her at the register, wielding a knife. "Give me some crosses!" he loudly demanded. Mary quickly complied. "I want more!" he screamed,

*The front counter at the Our Lady of Victory gift shop.*

brandishing his weapon towards her. At this point, the crook suddenly stopped talking. Perhaps something in the air shifted. Perhaps he caught the glowing light blazing at the corners of his eyes.

He slowly turned his head, cowering left and right. There in the far right corner of the gift store stood Nelson Baker, piercing his gaze directly into the man's eyes. In the far left corner stood a sight few on this earth have ever seen. It is a sight usually reserved only for combat with The Evil One and his minions. None other than St. Michael the Archangel was standing in the far left corner, decked out in full battle regalia with shining armor, a sword, and his massive "muscular" wings spread out to their full extent, his colossal frame towered up close to the ceiling. No doubt these two men could have quickly executed an effective pincers movement against this knife-wielding enemy, but no such action was required. The crook ran for the door as soon as he regained his senses, no doubt headed for the confessional booth upstairs. Apparently after the boy had left, Mary was able to briefly converse with Baker, even asking him "What are you doing here?" Yes, he had come to protect her.

There are some striking differences between these two stories to note such as the presence of a weapon, the appearance of St. Michael, the issue of where Father Baker stood during the event, if the youth jumped the counter, and if Baker lingered afterwards. It is difficult to attempt to discredit or corroborate any of this. How can you? Mary Timms is dead. There were no video cameras present, and likelihood of the thief surrendering himself at Lackawanna police headquarters remains as elusive as a Bills Super Bowl win. However, we do have two credible sources so we are as close to the truth as we are likely to get. As I said at the outset, my role is to deliver the facts, then allow the reader to delve into the area of belief.

However, there is one point that can be illuminated with a bit of context. That is the question of whether or not Baker lingered after the miracle was over. My guess would be that he did not. It would be out of character for him. In all of the miracles that he performed during his life, he always left quietly and immediately after they were finished, sometimes seemingly embarrassed. His humility is something few of us can grasp. Baker, like Christ, sought no self-aggrandizement or recognition for his deeds. He simply wanted to help people. For example, as chronicled in *Mysteries*, after he apparently raised the nurse "Miss Clark" from the dead at OLV Hospital, he silently slipped out of the room without a word. When a young girl rose from her wheelchair at the Blessed Sacrament Altar inside the Basilica, after Baker had healed her, the aging priest quietly left the church. Therefore, in all likelihood, Nelson Baker may have slipped in and out of time as quickly as he came.

Either way, he came to guard the young girl he met so many years ago, a girl named after the woman to whom he dedicated his life. No one would be allowed to injure her, or desecrate his shrine to Our Lady of Victory.

*Chapter Six:*
# THE HEALING VISION

The connections between Barbara Lawrence and Nelson Baker are striking. Lawrence was born in Corning, New York, in 1952. She lived in that southern New York State town for seven years during her childhood, even returning in the 1970s to visit St. Mary's Parish, where Father Baker spent his 39th year on this earth.[20]

Barbara is also a Civil War re-enactor. She serves in Company F of the 38th Regiment of Georgia Volunteer Infantry, and is a member of the Buffalo Civil War Roundtable. Lawrence explains wryly that she has both "Confederate and Yankee blood." Baker of course served in the Civil War, in June and July of 1863, as Robert E. Lee's army threatened the north. Baker was a volunteer in the 74th New York State Regiment of Militia. They saw action near Gettysburg, and in New York City.[21]

If Corning and the Civil War are not enough, Barbara's mother, Francis Page, knew Father Baker as a young girl who frequently visited St. Patrick's Church and later Our Lady of Victory Basilica. Francis would often tell her daughter all about her warm memories of visiting "Father Baker's." Born in 1908 into a Protestant family, Francis had to keep quiet about going to what her mother disdainfully called "*that* Church." Yet Francis went nonetheless. Her aunt had married a Roman Catholic. The members of that family were all parishioners and lived near the church. Francis spent a lot of her spare time with her cousins in Lackawanna and together they would go to Mass at St. Patrick's and later OLV. She even attended the dedication mass that officially opened the Basilica in 1925. Francis began to feel drawn to the pastor, insisting upon sitting in front during the services. She made a point of meeting Father Baker on several occasions after Mass, even shaking his hand once. She fondly recalled his soft spoken voice and gentle mannerisms. Page was of course there at Baker's funeral and wake in 1936, waiting in line for hours to kiss the ring on his finger.

As this young girl got older, got married, and gave birth to Barbara, she found herself drifting away from the Episcopal religion, as did her daughter. Seeking "more freedom of spiritual expression," mother and daughter both converted to Catholicism and became members of Our Lady of Victory Parish in 1978. They stayed members until Francis Page passed away on December 6, 2004. Her funeral was at the Basilica after which she was buried in nearby Holy Cross Cemetery, not far from Father Baker's original gravesite. Shortly after her mother's death in 2004, Barbara joined St. Thomas Aquinas Parish, near her home on Abbott Road.

These three intimate connections between Lawrence and Baker can hopefully inform our understanding of what took place in the basement of Our Lady of Victory Basilica in February 1999. It all began with an ear infection. Barbara was diagnosed as having a fluid build-up behind her ear and was immediately put on antibiotics in an attempt to clear this up. She was told that if the fluid did not go away, she would have to undergo an operation to remove the fluid. That was the last thing that this 46-year-old wanted to do. She had already gone through a slew of tests and procedures for various muscle disorders. "I was scared," she said. "I did not want to have the surgery."

Unfortunately for Barbara, the fluid did not go away. She was told to stop taking antibiotics for 30 days to clear her system, and to then see a specialist at ECMC to further diagnose and treat the lingering problem.

It was then that she turned to Father Baker. Barbara immediately began saying a novena to ask specifically for Baker's intercession to heal her. The power of novenas in connection with Nelson Baker was documented in *The Mysteries of Father Baker*. These nine day prayer sessions seem a potent mix of faith and the miraculous. Barbara Lawrence is certain that she completed at least one novena to Baker before the key day of Tuesday, February

*The 3"x 5" Civil War battle flag (middle) of Father Baker's 74th Regiment of New York State Militia stands wrapped around a nine foot staff inside a display case on the second floor of the Connecticut Street Armory in Buffalo. If Baker ever touched the flag it would be considered a second class relic.*

23, 1999, rolled around. This particular date was the night of her weekly prayer group meeting in the basement of Our Lady of Victory Basilica. The gathering met every Tuesday evening at the chapel just down the hall from the gift shop.

We should pause here to briefly note that February 23 is a date of singular importance on the Catholic liturgical calendar. This is the feast day of Saint Polycarp who died in Smyrna (in Western Asia Minor) on February 23, A.D. 155. This man, who knew the Apostle John, was one of the most hallowed saints in early Christendom. He refused to curse the Lord and refused to give praise to Caesar. The Romans then sentenced this distinguished 86 year-old bishop to be burned alive. However, Polycarp's body remained untouched when the fire was struck, as an arch of flames formed a protective wall around him. Frustrated, an executioner stepped forward and stabbed him to death. A narrative of his life and death circulated among early Christian groups and remains the "oldest account of Christian martyrdom outside the New Testament."[22] An annual festival to commemorate his life and death, which is still observed, "is the first regular commemoration of a martyr of which there is record."[23] February 23 has long been a day of power and pride for Catholics, especially in the early days of the Church.

This particular February 23 found Barbara Lawrence wrapping up her prayer session with the other members of the group just after 9 p.m. As was customary every week, each attendee had the option of staying a few minutes longer for the "Healing Ministry." Whoever chose to take part would walk over to the hallway in front of the Father Baker museum next to the gift shop, and gather for one final time before going home. This is only a short distance from the chapel. The idea was to then pray in unison to Father Baker to ask for his intercession to heal the intended person. This usually took only a few minutes.

Barbara made it known that she would like it if the group would pray for her this week so that her ear might be healed. As this group of five people began to pray, Barbara closed her eyes and joined them. They were all standing over her as she sat in a chair. Barbara prayed directly to Father Baker and asked him to heal her of this ear infection. All of sudden she began to feel heat on her head. That was odd. It was not there before. There was now an intense warmth that had centered like an arch over her head. Some other members of the group began to feel it too. The heat caused her to open her eyes and when she did they landed on a member of the group whom she did not notice before. In fact, no one else saw him.

Barbara had been praying with her head down, so the first thing that she saw about this man was his shoes. They were old and worn, "like my grandfather would have worn," she said. The owner of these shoes had done plenty of walking in them. As her eyes continued up she saw that he was short, frail, and wearing an antique looking black cassock and an angled priestly hat. His hat and vestments were trimmed in red, and he wore old-style spectacles. This priest was clearly in his 70s or 80s, and had a curious smile on his face. He said nothing, but his hands were extended over Barbara's head as he stood above her.

It was Father Baker.

Barbara then closed her eyes again. When she opened them back up moments later, the man was gone. Initially, she dismissed Baker as just one of the prayer group members. She questioned herself, saying that she barely knew these men and women, having joined just months before. Could it have just as easily been one of them?

Her opinion changed just weeks later when she was watching television with her mother. There was a report on the news about Father Baker. It just so happened that his body was being moved from Holy Cross Cemetery to the Basilica. The Vatican ordered this to allow more people to have easier access to his grave to seek his intercession for the miracle requirement for sainthood. When Barbara saw Baker's face on the television, she jumped out of her chair and said to her mother "Oh my God, that's him! That's the man who appeared to me at the healing ministry!" It was Father Nelson Baker.

This merely confirmed to her what she had already known on some level, that Baker had indeed healed her. Two days after this healing vision, Barbara had visited that specialist at ECMC and she was not surprised to find out that the fluid behind her ear had simply vanished. No further procedures or visits would be necessary regarding this matter. The news was not shocking to Barbara for one reason.

"I knew he (Baker) healed me the moment that it happened," she said. She did not really need the doctor to confirm this.

Barbara immediately knew that her story might be of interest to Our Lady of Victory Parish in the hope that this alleged miracle could move Father Baker further up the path to sainthood. As we will see in the final chapter "The Journey to Sainthood," this narrative seems to meet all of the miracle requirements. The healing was permanent, directly attributable to Father Baker, 100% in nature, and clear of any medicine or drugs that may have played a role in the recovery.

Monsignor Robert C. Wurtz, at that time the pastor of Our Lady of Victory Parish, saw to it that testimony was taken of the Lawrence case. Barbara even passed a psychological screening test mandated by Bishop Henry Mansell, who was then the head of the Buffalo Catholic Diocese. Mansell required that all prospective miracle cases include a psychological test to determine if mental illness is involved. Certainly the value of such a test is key in scientifically proving a potentially miraculous event. However, many have confided to me that such scrutiny is exactly what causes them to keep their stories unknown, anonymous, or incompletely told.

Nevertheless, Barbara Lawrence did not shy away from such intense examination. She embraced it, confident in the knowledge that what happened to her that February night in 1999 was indeed a miracle worked by the power of God through Nelson Baker.

Now we will have to see if the Vatican agrees.

*Chapter Seven:*
# THE NAME MIRACLE

One enduring legacy of Father Baker is the large number of people in Western New York to this very day who have named their sons after Nelson Henry Baker, using either his first name, or even his middle name. Floyd Anderson noted as much in his 1960 biography of the esteemed priest. "There is a mystery as to how Father Baker was given the first name of Nelson," Anderson wrote, a question that has still not been answered, and likely never will be. "There is none (however) as to why so many men in the Buffalo area bear it today."[24]

The name Nelson translates to "son of Neil," a name that in turn means "champion."[25] Therefore the literal translation of Nelson is "son of a champion." No meaning could be more fitting than for Nelson Smoczynski II, whose father is indeed a champion to his entire family, a living reminder of the power of Father Baker.

The connection between Nelson Baker and the Smoczynski family goes back to the early 20th Century. Nelson II's grandmother, Lillian, was born on June 15, 1919. As a young girl living in Dunkirk she quickly developed a devotion to Father Baker, praying to him after his death, and always coveting a gold Madonna statuette that she received in the mail from Our Lady of Victory in the early 1930s, likely blessed by the OLV pastor himself. (The figurine is still a coveted family heirloom.)[26]

As she grew older she was not surprised to be blessed with children. She eventually had four, even though doctors told her that she would be barren for her entire life. Her beloved husband, Daniel Smoczynski, a lifelong Dunkirk policeman, was a sergeant during World War II, but when he returned home from the Pacific, not all was right with him. He spent approximately the next 15 years in and out of veterans' hospitals. This put an enormous emotional and financial strain on the family, with Daniel unable to work at times. His own father had not enjoyed good health either, suffering from an advanced form of diabetes that had eaten away at his life and limbs. In fact, Daniel's father even had to have an entire leg amputated due to the ravishing effects of having "sugar."

By the spring of 1958, Daniel's situation had become critical. He was battling pneumonia, and he was losing. The war vet had tubes in his nose, an IV in his arm, and a loving wife always at his side. "He was dying from his head to his toes," said Nelson II. Doctors gave him no chance to live. They watched as the family priest performed the Last Rites on his near life-less body. Last Rites, also known as Extreme Unction, is a Catholic sacra-ment reserved for those on the very brink of death, used to absolve sin.

With nowhere else to turn, Lillian began to visit Our Lady of Victory Basilica. She did this nearly every day before going to the hospital to see her dying husband. She would light candles, pray, visit Baker's tomb at Holy Cross Cemetery, and ask Father Baker for a miracle. In a moment of inspi-ration she said to the late OLV pastor, "If you spare my husband, and we are somehow blessed with another child, I will name him in honor of you."

Sure enough, Daniel began to make nearly a full recovery. Not only that, Lillian was soon, amazingly, pregnant again. She gave birth to a healthy baby boy, Nelson Daniel Smoczynski, on March 29, 1959, just over two months shy of her 40th birthday.

Over the years, Daniel and Lillian frequently visited Our Lady of Victory to pray, light candles, and visit Father Baker's grave at Holy Cross Cemetery. The couple remained an active annual donor to the Our Lady Victory Parish endowment fund, right up until their final years. Daniel passed away on May 31, 1988, a full thirty years after his recovery. He had even been able to return to work in Dunkirk as a policeman. Lillian died on June 26, 2007, just over a week past her 88th birthday.

Throughout Lillian's long life, the story of her husband's recovery, the birth of her son, and the role that Father Baker had played in this drama was

*Lillian Smoczynski as she looked in her early 20s, in 1942.*

never far from her lips. It was a story that she retold to all who would listen, including her grandson, Nelson II, who was born on July 29, 1988, exactly 52 years after Father Baker's death. "I have always felt a special connection with him," he said, noting that he believes Nelson Baker got him through some tough times at St. Francis High School, including a potential brush with being expelled that surprisingly turned out just fine.

"I have his sense of kindness and self-giving," Nelson II said. He remembers calling on his namesake for help with a friend who was all but disowned by her family. "She was kicked out of the house by her parents." Unbeknownst to his destitute friend, Nelson paid a visit to Father Baker's tomb inside of Our Lady of Victory Basilica to ask for his help. "I told him that he had always helped my family so now I needed him to help another family," he said. The young man then felt inspired to pay a surprise visit to the girl's parents, a meeting that to this day the girl has no idea ever took place. The following day the family was back together. "Everything is better now," between the friend and her mother and her father, but Nelson is reluctant to acknowledge any role in the reconciliation, believing the true credit lies with the man who answered his prayers.

There is one chapter left to be written in this tale. One question still to be answered. So far, young Nelson is the second generation in the Smoczynski clan to carry on the name and legacy of Father Baker, now into the 21st Century. Will there be a third? If Nelson II ever had a son, would he name him Nelson? "Oh yes. I would have to," he said. Then thinking a moment, he added, "I would want to."

## *Chapter Eight:*
# THE STRANGE CASE OF DONALD HERBERT

It all began in December 1995. Thirty-three year-old Buffalo Firefighter Donald Herbert found himself in the worst situation imaginable, every firefighter's worst nightmare. He was trapped. The roof of the flaming house he had entered collapsed on Herbert, knocking him out and cutting off his air supply. As his fellow firemen desperately struggled to free and revive him, it became clear that Herbert had gone without oxygen for as long as 10 minutes. The Buffalo firefighter stayed in a coma for the next eight weeks, eventually settling into a "near persistent vegetative state,"[27] or a "minimally responsive state."[28]

He was not able to recognize any friends or relatives much less move, or communicate effectively for nearly a decade. Desperate for help, Herbert's wife, Linda, turned to Dr. Jamil Ahmed, a rehabilitation specialist at the Erie County Medical Center. For the next 24 months, Ahmed filled Donald Herbert with an endless stream of experimental drugs and therapies, none of which had any positive effect, as the Buffalo fireman continued to deteriorate. Finally, in February 2005, Ahmed tried yet another experimental drug cocktail designed to stimulate Herbert's neurotransmitters "which brain cells use to communicate with each other."[29] Significantly (as I will explain later) there was no measurable effect for weeks, until Saturday, April 30, 2005. Herbert was sitting in a wheelchair in the hallway of Father Baker Manor on Powers Road in Orchard Park when he suddenly began calling for his wife and his four sons.[30]

For the next 16 hours, Herbert was back to his old self, chatting with family and friends as if nothing had happened. Saying he felt "great,"[31] the fireman estimated he had been out for about three months, not ten years. Brain doctors could not recall any similar cases of people who had made such a remarkable recovery after so many years. He had no trouble counting or responding to simple commands. He looked like he was on the road to a full recovery.

With this goal in mind, the Herberts agreed to transfer him to a rehabilitation center in Chicago, but his condition began to worsen. The family decided to take him back home to Buffalo where he checked into the Ridge View Manor Nursing Home, and it quickly became clear that the Buffalo fireman was not doing well. He contracted pneumonia in February 2006, but his body did not respond to antibiotics. Less than a year after his dramatic recovery, Donald Herbert died in Buffalo Mercy Hospital on February 21, 2006, at approximately 2 a.m.[32]

Despite the untimely death of Donald Herbert, the question remains, was this a miracle? Certainly Dr. Eileen Reilly thought so. She was one of several physicians who took care of Herbert at Father Baker Manor. "I can't explain it any other way," she said at a press conference, just days after Herbert awoke from his persistent vegetative state. "It's phenomenal. It really is."[33]

Yet even if we can establish this as a miracle, exactly what role, if any, did Father Baker play in this case? Rumors of the family praying to Baker, and even using a piece of Baker's robe (2CR) to invoke the late mystic were rampant, including some made known to me personally on two separate occasions. Certainly the late Monsignor Robert Wurtz, pastor at OLV, wanted some answers from the family, but was willing to respect their privacy initially. "It's all speculation," he said.[34]

In answering these questions, let us use the rules that the Vatican employs to determine a miracle, because essentially those are the only ones that matter. First, there must be a direct line to Baker. If the family prayed to any other person than Baker, it is likely that this case would be rejected by the Vatican, because it would be theologically unclear who to give the proper "credit" for this intercession.

The second issue is whether Herbert completely recovered. Remember, the Vatican only accepts miracles that are 100 percent in nature, and have some permanence. This is where those crucial 16 hours when April turned into May in 2005 become critical. Herbert appeared to completely recover during this time period, and that may be just long enough. The *Catechism of the Catholic Church* defines a miracle as "a sign or wonder, such as a healing or the control of nature, which can only be attributed to divine power."[35] There is no mention of how long that "divine power" has to manifest Itself. Is not a miracle still a miracle even if it only lasts a few hours, or even a few seconds, as long as it cannot be explained by science?

This then leaves us with the most important question. Can this "miracle" be explained by science? Central to resolving this key issue is finding out the role that drugs played in the recovery of Donald Herbert. If the various drug cocktails administered to Herbert were responsible for his healing, then clearly divine credit can be ruled out.

There is one glaring aspect to this case that seems to favor the miraculous, and not the scientific. Herbert was administered "a new combination of drugs"[36] in February 2005. And nothing happened. He stayed in his near persistent vegetative state for another three months. It was not until April 30, 2005, that he came out of his near persistent vegetative state, long after those drugs would have left his circulatory system. The lag time is crucial. If Herbert had awoken within hours, or even days, after being administered these new drugs, that would at least indicate a strong correlation between the drugs and his recovery. The lag time gives any potential correlation less strength and the possibility of a miracle even more likelihood.

Let us then begin to examine the potential role of the supernatural in this case. First, there could not be a better day for renewal and recovery than the magical day of April 30, the day Herbert emerged from his minimally responsive state. In Celtic lore, April 30 is known as "Bealtaine," or "May Eve." It is a fire and fertility festival of renewal, as the sun is "coaxed"[37] to bring its nourishing and healing warmth back to the earth. This day, the calendar's opposite of Halloween, is celebrated in many cultures including the German, the Scottish, and the Welsh. It denotes the commencement of the growing season, and is usually accompanied by celebrations and bonfires.

Was this unique day of renewal and healing touched by Father Baker as well? We must answer what role he played in this story. There essentially are two possibilities to show a connection to Baker in this case, besides the fact that it took place at Father Baker Manor. Was any relic of Baker's used, such as dirt from his former grave, or a piece of his clothing? Or did the family pray directly to him for his intercession? Both in fact seem to be the case, and were discussed in the 2007 book *The Day Donny Herbert Woke Up* written by journalist Rich Blake.

In this book, Blake chronicled several connections to Baker including the following:

- Herbert attended Baker Victory High School.[38]
- Msgr. Wurtz placed a cross owned by Baker over Herbert's body in February 1996.[39]
- Herbert claimed that he saw Baker in his room at Baker Manor.[40]
- Family members prayed to Baker, including at Our Lady of Victory Basilica.[41]

Blake also reported that Wurtz concluded that the drug cocktail was the reason for the recovery, not Father Baker, and the pastor chose not to pursue the matter any further.[42] Although the connection was not made in the book, another reason Wurtz may have called off any investigation might have been an insurmountable fact that was all too clear to such a veteran of the canonization process. According to Blake, Linda Herbert "had prayed to every saint and holy figure on record."[43] The Vatican would take one look at this reality and run the other way. Even if a miracle could be proved in this case, there would be no way to determine who to "credit" the miracle to. As we noted, there must be a direct, clear line to Baker, which is not present in this case.

Such details matter little to the Herbert family. Whatever the reason for Herbert's recovery, be it Father Baker or otherwise, the fact remains that they got back a father and a husband, even if it was just for a short whisper in time.

*Chapter Nine:*
# THE TRIO MIRACLE

David Hatten keeps it in his wallet. This small piece of metal is a constant reminder of the power of a man he is convinced helped to save his life. That man is, of course, Father Baker, and the item in question is a miraculous medal with Baker's image on it, given to him by a neighbor years ago. Technically the article is not a relic of the late OLV pastor, since it was never owned, touched, or even blessed by him, but that hardly matters in the Hatten family.[44]

This story begins in 1994 when Dave met his future wife, Deborah, whom he married the following year. The dream that any couple shares for a long and healthy life together was quickly put on hold when Dave experienced kidney failure shortly after their nuptials. The trouble centered on a rare condition known as "amyloidosis." This disorder is caused by:

> *abnormal folding of proteins...These clumps of proteins are called amyloid deposits and the accumulation of amyloid deposits causes the progressive malfunction and eventual failure of the affected organ (in this case the kidneys). Normally proteins are broken down at about the same rate as they are produced, but these unusually stable amyloid deposits are deposited more rapidly than they can be broken down. The accumulation may be localized in one organ or may be systemic such that several organs are affected.[45]*

Stated simply, David's kidneys were not breaking down protein well enough. Hatten was then placed on dialysis, which is a time consuming, costly, cumbersome treatment regimen designed to restore proper balance to the blood.[46]   Dialysis however is no cure. It just buys some time. To ensure a higher survival rate, and a better quality of life, a kidney transplant must be sought immediately for patients suffering from kidney disease.

For an entire year, the Hatten clan went through the expensive, protracted process of searching for a donor. The key was to find the right match; a kidney with a similar composition to David's to ensure that his body would not reject the new organ. The natural place to look first for a donor is among family members, who have similar DNA. The Hattens were devastated and surprised to find out that not a single member of the family was a good enough match. Prospects began to look quite bleak, until Deborah offered herself to be tested. Could it be that this couple who had already shared so much could literally be a perfect match for each other? Amazingly, the answer was yes. The operation began in short order to remove David's malfunctioning kidneys and replace them with Deborah's healthy one.

Throughout the ordeal, the family prayed to three people. They would be the trio whom they would turn to in times of need, keeping them strong through the hardest of times that still lay ahead. This all-star lineup included Saint Jude, the patron saint of lost causes, the Blessed Virgin Mary, and of course Father Nelson Baker. Why Baker? Essentially because the family heard reports in the media and in the community about Baker having the power to heal people, and the Hattens were seeking any help they could get.

We should pause however to recall a harsh reality that we alluded to in the "Coma Miracle" above. The fact that the family prayed to three people is a theological dead-end for the miracle requirement to move a candidate up the path to sainthood. The Vatican would say in such a case as this that any alleged miracle is not even worth investigating because it is unclear who was responsible for the supposed healing. Was it Saint Jude? Was it Nelson Baker? Was it Mary? Was it all three, or perhaps a combination of two? There is no way of knowing, save for a Tesla telephone to the dead. We, however, will continue our exploration of this matter if for no other reason than the family involved believes strongly in the role that Baker played in the case. They are the guideposts here that we will follow.

Much to the relief of David and his wife, he took well to the new kidney. He did have a mild "episode of rejection" two years later, but he pulled through with more prayer and medication as his body continued to adjust to the new organ. All seemed back to normal for about five years after that brief scare came and went in 1998. The couple settled into the routine of married life that really had been denied to them for so long.

Then suddenly in 2003 David Hatten's situation became critical. His fever spiked unexpectedly, which was a clear sign of trouble. He was rushed to the hospital and after being tested got perhaps the worst news of his life. What had caused his kidney failure so many years before had now returned in his new kidney, a dangerous build-up of protein. Also, David found out that his doctors had misdiagnosed him years ago. In 1996, his physicians thought that he had the highly treatable "secondary" amyloidosis, which "occurs in association with another disease."[47] If doctors can identify this other disease, they can treat the patient successfully. As it turns out David also had Crohn's Disease, which his doctors pinpointed at the time as the likely culprit causing secondary amyloidosis. Crohn's Disease is:

> *a chronic inflammatory disease of the intestines. It primarily causes ulcerations (breaks in the lining) of the small and large intestines, but can affect the digestive system anywhere from the mouth to the anus... Crohn's Disease is related closely to another chronic inflammatory condition that involves only the colon called ulcerative colitis...Ulcerative colitis and Crohn's Disease have no medical cure. Once the diseases begin they tend to fluctuate between periods of inactivity (remission) and activity (relapse).*[48]

Hatten's medical team was puzzled that the protein build-up had returned in 2003, assuming that they had solved this issue years ago with a kidney transplant. In fact, all they had done was buy David some more time. All those years, unbeknownst to the Hattens, or his doctors, he was suffering from "primary" amyloidosis, its most deadly form. Primary is "caused by an abnormal plasma cell in the bone marrow."[49] This would continue to affect him no matter how many kidney transplants he received. Primary amyloidosis, like Crohn's Disease, has no cure. It can only be treated.

With two developing problems now affecting his health, the only chance David had was to undergo a risky, experimental procedure at Roswell Park Hospital. Hatten underwent a bone marrow transplant using stem cells from his own body. This procedure was developed by Martha Skinner of Boston University. It does not cure the patient of amyloidosis, but instead is used in an attempt to treat the effects of having the disease. Hatten was then given chemo therapy as his wife watched him wither away, day after day. His body rejected the chemicals, and his blood count got dangerously low. Months later, Hatten's doctors would confide to Deborah that they did not expect him to live. At the time though, his physicians were coy, saying only that "things were touchy." In fact, David Hatten was rapidly dying.

As she had done years before after her husband's transplant operation, Deborah turned in desperation and faith to her divine trio yet again, but this time using a Father Baker medal given to her by her neighbor, Kathy Kessler. Her prayers were answered. David unexpectedly made a full recovery, returning from the depths of death itself. The bone marrow transplant worked. Not only that, every year since the surgery he has visited his doctor for his annual checkup, and each year since 2004 he has been given a clean bill of health. No episodes with rejection, no relapses, and hopefully no new worries. Amazingly, there have been no new signs of either Crohn's Disease, or primary amyloidosis.

Even though events have conspired to work out so well for David and Deborah, they have not ceased praying, stopping twice a day to reflect in moments of thanksgiving. As far as Nelson Baker's part in ensuring the survival and good health of her husband, Deborah is convinced that Baker had a "big role in this," she said with confidence. "Of that I have no doubt."

## *Chapter Ten:*
# THE GIFT OF SANCTUARY

The central figure in this story has chosen to remain anonymous. We will respect her wishes and only use her first name, Jen, and provide just the essential facts. She was so profoundly touched by what happened to her at Our Lady of Victory Basilica in 2006 that it is still difficult for her to fully talk about it years later. Jen believes that the events surrounding this narrative are a private matter between herself and God and go far deeper than she has ever been able to express or share with anyone. Not only that, the actions she felt compelled to take on faith are somewhat controversial in the Catholic Church. However, her courage in coming forward may help to show the scope of God's power working through Nelson Baker. The details are actually quite simple and brief when put into words, but complex and enduring when imprinted on a human soul.

There are an abundance of surprising facts to this case that on the surface would never lead us to believe that Father Baker would be in any way connected to it. Jen is not Catholic. She is Methodist. Jen did not have any special devotion or family connections to Father Baker. In fact she never even heard about him growing up in Oklahoma. There are also no relics involved with this case that could be traced back to the OLV pastor, nor any novenas directed towards heaven. Instead, all we seem to have is fate.[50]

Jen's odyssey that would lead to Our Lady of Victory Basilica began with some bad news. She found out after a series of tests and scans that she had lesions all over her liver. These were most likely the telltale signs of deadly liver cancer. She was scheduled for a biopsy to remove and test a sample of the liver on Friday, September 15, 2006.

Before she went for surgery that day she had a stop to make. This Oklahoma native had recently become friends with a fellow parishioner at her Methodist church named Carol, who came from a Catholic family. Carol knew all about the alleged miracle-working ability of Father Baker from local folklore, and media reports. She also knew that her friend might have cancer. Together they decided to make a trip to Our Lady of Victory to pray before the operation took place and seek out the help of the Lackawanna mystic.

As Jen walked in the door of the Basilica, she was stunned. She had never seen a place of worship like this, nor had she ever felt such a sense of comfort, tranquility, and peace in her entire life. This was truly sacred ground. She began to feel overwhelmed emotionally by the religious imagery and riot of colors inside the church. The two women arrived during Mass, and Jen did not think twice about getting in line for Communion. In the Methodist Church, she explained, all people are welcome to receive the offering, not just Methodists. Jen innocently had little idea that her taking of the Body and Blood of Christ was strictly prohibited because she was not Catholic.

The Catholic Catechism is clear on this point in stating that Protestants "have not preserved the proper reality of the Eucharistic mystery in its fullness, especially because of the absence of the sacrament of Holy Orders. It is for this reason that, for the Catholic Church, Eucharistic intercommunion with these communities is not possible."[51]

After Mass, the two women made a point to pray in front of Father Baker's grotto to ask for his help and comfort. This was also something new for Jen. The idea of saints and intermediaries to intercede on your behalf in front of God was a foreign concept to this Methodist. Yet Jen found herself doing it anyway. There was such a sense of comfort and belonging in this church that she had not expected. In her time of fear and need she had found a place of spiritual refuge, as had many Protestants whom Father Baker had welcomed into his institutions during his life. Perhaps this was because Baker's own father, Lewis, was a Protestant. At the very least, Baker spent part of his early life exposed to his father's Lutheran faith. To this day, Baker Victory Services prides itself on helping people of all religions in its group homes.

After Mass and reflection at the grotto, she was ready to face her biopsy with a renewed courage. After a weekend of more prayer and anxiety, the following Monday evening, September 18, the test results came in from the biopsy. Something odd had happened. There was no cancer in her liver. Everyone was surprised and relieved at this strange news.

*Author's personal collection*

*Nelson Baker's final resting place inside Our Lady of Victory Basilica.*

The obvious question then is, did Father Baker heal Jen from her liver cancer so that none was found when the biopsy was performed? It is very hard to answer this definitively. We do not know for example (nor can we ever know), if there was cancer in the liver before the test. If cancer was definitely in the liver before the biopsy, then she prayed to Baker at OLV, and then a test performed just hours later came back negative, it would seem evident that a miracle had taken place. The only sticking point is that we cannot prove years later if there actually was cancer in that liver beforehand. Jen's doctors thought there probably was. If that was true there would be no scientific explanation for cancer disappearing that quickly after praying at Our Lady of Victory.

The possibility of being healed by Father Baker is not the most important point of this trial for Jen. Far more crucial was her finding sanctuary in a place that she had never been before, and in a man she knew preciously little about.

"I honestly don't know if I was healed," Jen said. "I never asked to be healed. I asked for God's will to be done. I know that God listened to me and helped me." As far as Baker goes, Jen believes that he provided her with reassurance and hope that she would get through the ordeal. "Just going to the Basilica was great comfort," she said. "It gave me a lot of peace."

Perhaps not surprisingly, Jen would not be the only one seeking peace at Nelson Baker's shrine to his beloved Our Lady of Victory. An aging war veteran and his daughter were in search of this same gift from Father Baker when they arrived there six years earlier.

*Chapter Eleven:*
# THE PEACE MIRACLE

Robert Fire had seen his fair share of suffering. As a World War Two veteran he had served with distinction in the Battle of the Bulge, one of the most protracted, deadliest battles of that war. He had also seen his wife, Mabel, suffer through a long, painful death as she lingered week after week in her hospital bed after suffering a stroke. Meanwhile the family seemed helpless in their efforts to comfort her as she passed away.

Yet throughout the various tribulations of his life, Fire and his loved ones consistently turned to Father Nelson Baker for help. The family regularly attended Mass at the Basilica, and always felt his presence in their lives. Robert even prayed to the late OLV pastor during his time oversees, as did his entire family. The Fires were convinced that the Lackawanna prelate had protected their father from harm, and had ensured his safe return home.[52]

As their father began to get older, two of Robert's children, Mrs. Brenda Flateau, and Mrs. Marie Sommer, started to become particularly concerned that he would not suffer from the same fate as their mother. They wanted to make sure that when the time came, he would have a peaceful, dignified death. Fire's 81st birthday was quickly approaching on Thursday, November 16, 2000, so Brenda figured that there was no time to waste in beginning to prepare for this inevitability. The weekend before his birthday, Brenda got her father to agree to accompany her to the Basilica to pray for this special favor at Father Baker's newly installed grotto. They would do this before attending Mass and make a day of it.

Robert Fire agreed to go. The father/daughter duo set out for the Basilica on the morning of Saturday, November 11, 2000. Incidentally, November 11 is considered by many people to be a particularly sacred, holy day. The date, of course, is 11/11 on the calendar – all "ones." One is the most divine of numbers, symbolizing unity, harmony, and the one true God. It is also a day of peace, the very thing that Robert Fire and Brenda Flateau were seeking that day. History even points to this on at least two significant occasions. The Treaty of Canandaigua, also known as the Pickering Treaty, was signed on November 11, 1794, by the representatives of the Unites States government and various chiefs of the Iroquois Confederacy.[53] This agreement brought peace to these two sides in the years following the American Revolution, during which the Iroquois had suffered horribly from the Sullivan Campaign. Also, on November 11, 1918, at 11 am, World War I came to an end as the Allies and the Central Powers signed an armistice to close what was at that time the most destructive war in human history.

As the duo made their way into the church, Brenda went right to the grotto to pray directly in front of Nelson Baker's remains. Somehow during her intense reflection and praying she lost track of time, and her father. She looked all over the church, but simply could not find him. Eventually she got the idea to check outside and of course there he was, waiting for her patiently. He had something important to share with her.

> *"I don't have to go to Mass today," he said with a wry smile.*
> *"And why not?" Brenda asked, incredulously.*
> *"Because the priest inside said that I don't have to," Fire explained.*
> *"And why did he say that?" Brenda pressed him.*
> *"Because he gave me Communion."*

Now Brenda was a little bit puzzled. This seemed unusual on a Saturday morning. "What priest gave you communion?" she demanded. Her father then proceeded to describe in detail a short, frail, old priest with long, flowing vestments (that priests typically wore before Vatican II). He was giving her an exact description of Father Nelson Baker. They went back inside and looked everywhere, but they could not seem to find anyone, priest or otherwise, to fit this description. Her father was insistent however, and could not get over how good he was feeling. In any event, whoever had just given her father the Eucharist had simply disappeared.

Marie Sommer remembers the days and weeks following this mysterious incident as one of particular joy for her father. He seemed at peace with himself, and his life. His birthday came and went without incident, but then on Thanksgiving Day, November 23, he said something odd. His daughter Marie reminded him that she was going on a skiing trip over the weekend, and that she looked forward to seeing him when she got back.

> *"No, I don't think so," he said, quite seriously.*
> *"Oh, don't be silly, Dad," Marie said, a bit shocked. "We'll see you when we get back."*
> *"No," he said. "I am ready to die."*

Robert Fire somehow knew that it was his time. When they found his body on Sunday, November 26, it looked as if he had just drifted off into a restful sleep. Everyone remarked upon the unusual tranquility and look of peace that pervaded his face. The gift of a quiet, dignified death that Brenda Flateau had so ardently prayed for just two weeks before had been granted. And there was no doubt as to whom the family believed was responsible for this divine favor.

"We truly believe that he was visited by Father Baker," said Marie Sommer. Certainly apparitions of Father Baker are not unknown in the Basilica, as we noted in the "Ghostly Miracle." Such stories suggest that the power of this man extends far beyond the grave, and death itself has done nothing to impede his miracle-working capacity, including appearing and interacting in bodily form on this earth.

What may be equally impressive however is that this event was apparently not the last time that this special family was touched by the miraculous, posthumous, work of Nelson Baker. Less than two years later, this same family turned again to the very man who had just helped their father pass into the beyond. Could he come through for them yet again?

*Chapter Twelve:*
# THE MIRACLE OF THE SACRED GROUND

While growing up in Kenmore, New York, Marilyn Sheriff prided herself on her strong Catholic upbringing. She and her close-knit family always felt that their faith was one of their most cherished gifts, especially after her mother, Jackie, passed away in 1995. Marilyn can fondly recall family outings to visit many of the local Catholic parishes. These usually included her own parish, St. Paul's, and frequent trips to two local Catholic mainstays, Lewiston's Fatima Shrine to the Blessed Virgin Mary, and of course Lackawanna's Our Lady of Victory Basilica. OLV was of special significance to the Sheriff family because Marilyn's paternal grandmother, Theresa Sheriff, was acquainted with Father Baker as a young girl, having gone to school at Baker's institutions.[54]

However, as many young people who grow up in Western New York find out, prospects are often more promising elsewhere. Before long, she was calling Delaware her new home state. It would be here, on an overpass just off Route 95 in Wilmington, that her life would change forever.

The date was December 14, 2002, at 5 a.m. The day had yet to dawn, leaving the frigid roads pitch black. Driving alone along her usual route to work, this 20 year-old young woman was expecting little difficulty this particular morning, except perhaps the occasional early commuter, or some interstate truckers. The exact details of what happened this morning remain sketchy even years later. Under the threat of being sued, the Sheriff family has spent thousands of dollars hiring experts to reconstruct this horrible day, and all they essentially came back with were more questions and few answers. Part of the problem was a lack of many witnesses. For example, Marilyn herself remembers precious little of the entire episode.

However, we do know a few details about that morning from the work of police, family, and friends. Marilyn Sheriff's tiny sports car slammed headlong into a bus. The bus was filled with senior citizens on their way to various morning appointments. Most of them died. The collision was so violent that death likely occurred on impact. We also know that an anonymous caller phoned 911 just moments after the collision, and for some reason he has never come forward, or been identified. His presence at the scene seems odd, and unlikely, but he somehow was in the right place at the right time to get an ambulance on the scene immediately. Then he disappeared into the blackness.

EMS arrived at the site and began to frantically work on Sheriff. She was unconscious, and barely alive with severe head trauma. While still at the scene, Sheriff remembers having what she calls an "out of body experience." She can recall physically walking up to the emergency medical staff and asking them if they needed help. She even remembers walking among the crowd of onlookers, and near the car wreck, seeking a way to be of some assistance. She did not see who was injured. These could not be conscious memories from her at the accident scene since she was unconscious at the time, and therefore would not have been able to recall these details of the scene, or the faces of the people attempting to revive her. Instead, these "memories" may in fact indicate, in the view of some, that her soul had indeed left her body and that she was quite near to death.

When Marilyn Sheriff arrived at nearby Christiana Hospital, after a desperate high-speed race against death along the local roads, her situation was critical. Marilyn's older sister, Melody, a 23 year-old nurse at the hospital, was contacted as the next of kin. She gave authorization to do all that was necessary to save her sister's life. It was clear that extraordinary measures would have to be taken. As she was put in the Intensive Care Unit, Marilyn's doctors decided to keep her in a coma for as long as needed. It was clear that the young woman had a severe and traumatic brain injury, and that a blood clot had formed in the brain. Doctors immediately began open skull surgery to remove the clot. This is a very delicate operation. Removing the clot can often mean disturbing the brain or even removing part of the brain attached to the clot. A full blood transfusion was given. A tracheotomy was performed.

When the exhausting procedure was completed, Sheriff's doctors were quite pessimistic. Marilyn's father, John, was on vacation in Asia and was told by the medical staff that it would not be necessary for him to rush home. His daughter would likely die quite soon. But instead, this young woman somehow lingered on. Several times she flat-lined, and nurses had to rush in to restart her heart. Later, the nursing staff would admit that they had never worked harder and longer on anyone.

Word quickly began to spread about her condition. A barrage of prayers was sent heavenward by family and friends. John Sheriff enlisted the support of some Buddhist friends in Asia. One of Marilyn's friends, Deborah Jewels, a Protestant minister at a local Evangelical Church, prayed over her body. Marilyn's boyfriend, Stephen Episcopo, prayed for her every day, as did countless other friends, family, and even hospital staff. Still the situation remained bleak. Sheriff's doctors insisted that even if she managed to come out of the coma, she would be paralyzed, or mentally disabled. There was no way that she could possibly be the same person that she was before the accident.

Back in Western New York, Marilyn's aunt, Marie Sommer, decided that she needed to take action. She would turn again to the man whom she had prayed to her entire life, a man who brought her father back home from World War II and had eased him peacefully into the next life. It was time to call on the help of Father Nelson Baker.

Marie Sommer made a trip to Holy Cross Cemetery to visit a certain location known to her since her childhood, the original grave of the Lackawanna prelate. From 1936 to 1999, Baker's remains were interred with his parents at this sprawling cemetery that is adjacent to the Basilica. As we noted, Baker's body was moved into the church in 1999. Still, his remains did reside in this ground for 63 years, during which time three vials of his blood did not decay and still behaved as if it was inside of his body.

To many people, Baker's former gravesite, still the resting place of his parents, remains quite holy. "I believe it is sacred ground," said Marie Sommer.[55] Marie decided to take a sample of this soil (3CR) and mail it to her niece, Melody, who agreed to place it under the bed of her sister, and see to it that it stayed right there.

*Author's personal collection*

*Baker's original gravesite in Holy Cross Cemetery, Lackawanna. Even though his remains have not been under this ground since 1999, many still believe that the soil is sacred. This photo from the summer of 2008 shows evidence of soil collection in front of the tombstone.*

After a total of two and a half weeks, Marilyn came out of the coma. Although it was not immediately clear, Sheriff's doctors were stunned to discover that she did not have a trace of any physical or mental disabilities. It did take some hard work to regain her proper speech patterns (typical for coma victims), but today Marilyn shows little signs of the accident that changed her life, except for the scars. When she meets new people, especially those in the medical field, they stare at her in disbelief when she tells them her story and how she suffered from severe head trauma and recovered without a trace. It is at that point that she shows them the scars on her head from the open skull surgery, or the scars on her stomach, evidence of the cutting needed to stop her internal bleeding.

Marilyn Sheriff is now an aspiring actress, planning a move to Los Angeles. She has been in three films sponsored by Temple University, helped with production for *Spiderman 3*, and has also won awards from the Modeling Association of America.

Still, the question for us is "what role did Father Baker play in this?" Yes, the Vatican would point out that many people in this case prayed to various sources, the theological sticking point that we encountered in the "Coma Miracle," for example. Yet it was only the sacred earth of Baker's grave that remained with her constantly. No other relics were employed. Is it just a coincidence that Marilyn only recovered and came out of the coma after the sacred Baker soil showed up, and not before? Why were other prayers seemingly not working until that soil showed up?

Certainly, Marilyn herself believes that Baker played a "huge role" in her recovery, as does Marie Sommer. Marie told her niece constantly during the hard times of her adjustment period after the accident that Father Baker was with her and that she would continue to pray to him. Even though the doctors were so wrong about their prognosis, they were right about one thing regarding Marilyn Sheriff. Yes, if she survived, she would not be the same person that she was before the accident.

"I know now that I have to do something important with my life," she said with determination. "I feel closer to God now than I have ever been in my life."

*Chapter Thirteen:*
# THE MIRACLE OF ONE

As an American History professor at St. Francis High School, Mr. Timothy Ellis is well aware of the importance of the date November 11. As we noted above, it is remembered as a day of peace because it brought an end to the carnage of the "Great War" in 1918, and peace to the Iroquois after the American Revolution. It is also revered by many as a blessed day because of the symbolism of the one true God embodied in the number one. But for our purposes, it was the day in the year 2000 when Nelson Baker apparently appeared to Robert Fire inside Our Lady of Victory Basilica.

Exactly a year later, as all the ones lined up across the calendar again, including even the year itself (11/11/01), Father Baker was called on again, but this time in an entirely different case. Could he save a dying woman fighting for her life inside the hospital founded by the Sisters of Mercy? Could the magic of this hallowed day be invoked once more? The woman in question was Mrs. Elizabeth Ellis, Timothy's wife of 29 years. This particular Sunday was their anniversary.[56]

The day began like any other. Tim Ellis was on his way back from Rushford Lake taking care of some family business and looking forward to spending some time with his beloved Liz on this long Veterans' Day weekend. Monday beckoned as a relaxing day off from the usual routine at school.

On the way back from the Southern Tier to his home in Blasdell, Ellis had planned to get off at the Hamburg exit on Route 219 to visit his parents, but as he approached the turn-off, something inside him knotted up.

Perhaps he could visit them tomorrow. For some reason he needed to get home. Fast.

As he bounded in the front door of his house, Ellis tried to stay calm, but something was just not right. Everything was a bit too quiet for this late in the day. It was already about 11 a.m. His thoughts immediately went to finding Liz. He had been worried about her lately. Her kidneys had been acting up again.

This was nothing new for Elizabeth Ellis. She had endured kidney stones nearly her entire life. In fact just the week before, she went into convulsions during a kidney stone attack. She was even given a stent that was placed in her bladder to help pass the stone, and then sent home. The Tuesday after Veterans' Day she was scheduled for a lithotripsy to blast any remaining stones out of the bladder. Liz had even gone home early from work on Friday because she felt so weak.

All this was racing through Tim Ellis' thoughts as he searched the house. He hurriedly glanced into the bedroom. No one. He checked the computer room. Again, no one. Was she outside? No. Perhaps he would check one more time upstairs. In his haste, did he somehow overlook where she was? Sure enough, when he reentered their bedroom his eyes fell upon a sight that will likely remain etched in his memory forever.

There she was, sitting on the floor with a strange vacancy in her eyes, staring into nothing, mumbling nonsense. Elizabeth had clearly fallen over for some reason, knocked over the end table on her way down, and sent books and Gatorade spilling everywhere. Tim Ellis hurriedly called 911. When emergency personnel arrived, they immediately began working on her as the ambulance raced to Mercy Hospital in South Buffalo. Upon arrival, Elizabeth was whisked away, leaving Ellis little to do but pace the ER waiting room. Forty-five minutes later, a welcome visitor stepped in the door - his daughter, Kristin. Together they received the first piece of bad news for the day.

"We have the chaplain coming," one of the emergency room doctors told them. Immediately, Ellis knew what this meant. They had informed him of the same thing just before his father-in-law passed away at Mercy just recently. This soft speaking doctor suggested that father and daughter relocate to the Bereavement Room and await the minister's arrival. This could of course mean only one thing. The hospital staff expected Liz to die, if she had not in fact died already.

A short time later another emergency room doctor tracked down the Ellis family and stated plainly "I do not think she will live." Elizabeth had suffered a stroke. The death process was beginning. She was in a coma, her muscles were deteriorating, and her kidneys were malfunctioning. Then the neurologist on staff confirmed this within the same hour, telling Ellis directly "I do not think she will make it." Unknown to Tim Ellis at that moment, but upon arrival Elizabeth's cousin, Carol, a registered nurse, was given the same devastating information by the hospital staff. She stiffly informed them that such news should give them no excuse to give up on her. Now that was four different doctors with the same diagnosis: imminent death.

No one in the Ellis family was giving in yet, especially Liz's mother, Dorothy. She showed up at the hospital armed with two Father Baker relics that she was ready to place directly on her dying daughter. Both of these relics can easily be traced to Father Baker himself. Before we move ahead in the story, let us then pause to first establish the authenticity of these relics, and explain where they came from.

The first item is a handkerchief. This white cloth was placed on the hands of Nelson Baker during his wake by Elizabeth's grandmother, Mary Frankenberger Wehrfritz, on August 1, 1936. This was typical for the days after Baker's death as his body lay in state and hundreds of thousands of mourners lined the streets of Lackawanna to pay their last respects. As they passed by, most touched his hands, leaving the gloves worn to the bone by the time Baker's body was interred. We discussed the miracles surrounding his wake and burial in *The Mysteries of Father Baker*. This particular cloth (3CR) was given by Mrs. Wehrfritz to her daughter, Dorothy, for safe-keeping. Today it is in the possession of Mrs. Ellis, but in a smaller form. Over the years the cloth has been cut into smaller pieces and given to various people seeking the intercession of Father Baker.

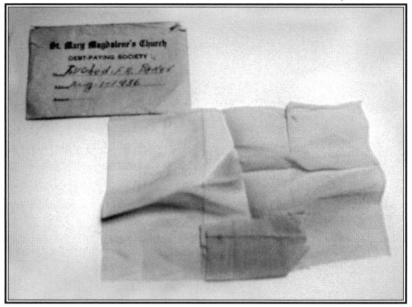

*The white handkerchief touched to Baker's hands at his funeral that was placed on Elizabeth Ellis.*

The second relic is much more complex in its description and origin. It is a purple colored piece of fabric known as a rabbi. We will discuss this particular priestly vestment in more detail in the next section. The story of how this item got into the hands of Dorothy Roehling, Liz's mother, begins with a fairly benign explanation. A cleaning woman whose name is lost to history was apparently going through some of Father Baker's tattered, old garments when she asked him what he would like her to do with them. He simply told her to "throw them out." However, instead of discarding them, which she felt would be disrespectful to this holy man, she kept them. This cleaning woman then turned them over to a trusted friend, Sister Mary Clarence, a Sister of St. Joseph, who worked at the orphanages. Sister Mary Clarence later became good friends of the Frankenberger family through her friendship with Father Florien Frankenburger, an uncle of Elizabeth's who was an educator at Canisius High School and a priest at St. Anne's Parish. Sister Mary Clarence gave away many pieces of this rabbi over the years, including a small section to Mary Frankenberger Wehrfritz. As we noted above, Elizabeth's grandmother was a devotee of Nelson Baker, waiting in line for hours to touch her handkerchief to his hands. She was likely a natural fit for Sister Clarence to give a piece of this sacred garment to. After Wehrfritz passed away, the handkerchief and the rabbi came into the possession of Dorothy Roehling, Mrs. Ellis' mother.

It was these two items that Dorothy Roehling brought with her to Mercy Hospital on the night of Sunday, November 11, 2001. She had one goal in mind: to get them onto the body of her daughter as quickly as possible. Fortunately, the nursing staff was more than accommodating to her wishes. Both items were taped to Elizabeth's leg and the nurses made sure the relics stayed there constantly. They were not to be tampered with or removed under any circumstances.

Meanwhile, Tim Ellis kept up his prayer vigil in the hospital chapel, praying to Father Baker. By this time he had contacted several friends and family. "I had just about everybody praying to Father Baker," said Ellis. One of the people he called was Father Joseph Benicewicz, a teacher and administrator at St. Francis High School. The Franciscan agreed to come down to Mercy and give Elizabeth the Last Rites, the Catholic Sacrament reserved for those on the very brink of death.

Then as night stretched into morning on the 12th, something odd happened. Elizabeth did not die. She fought on. Still, the doctors were pessimistic. The family doctor showed up, took one look at Mrs. Ellis, and began to tear up. At 9 a.m. another neurologist stopped by and repeated the same prognosis that the family had heard the day before. Slowly, the realization of the extreme gravity of this situation was beginning to sink in for Ellis. "I thought, 'Am I ever going to see her again? Am I ever going to talk to her again?' And all of this on our 29th wedding anniversary."

As the second day of the crisis lingered on, a breakthrough on Monday night tore a hole into the dire predictions of the hospital staff, and sent everyone's emotions soaring. At around 6 p.m. Mrs. Ellis regained consciousness. She was responding to some basic stimuli by shaking her head and squeezing her husband's hand. By Tuesday night, although still weak, she was able to talk again. Tim Ellis was enraptured by this sudden turn off events, this roller coaster of emotions sending him to the depths of despair and to the height of joy. "She was alive!" he says with incredulity even years later.

Alive, but not out of the woods yet. One problem was that her vision in the left eye had not fully returned. Another setback was that she could not walk. And if that was not bad enough, what about those lingering kidney stones that likely played a role in putting her in the hospital in the first place? Finally, would there be any permanent neurological damage?

To sort these issues out, Elizabeth was sent to the stroke unit at Our Lady of Victory Hospital where she said she felt more "at home." In a turning point moment she refused to sign papers to receive Social Security. The staff there assumed she would be permanently disabled and would never be able to go back to work full time, much less walk again.

With more prayer and more determination, Mrs. Ellis was back on her feet. We should note, however, that in 2008 she was still walking with a limp and experienced pain in her left leg. However, she could move the left leg and foot quite well, and can even cross the left leg over her right leg.

Within a few months, Mrs. Ellis' vision also was restored, but it did look for a while that her kidneys were about to shut down, and that she would have to be put on the expensive, time consuming treatment of dialysis. Just before this option was going to be exercised, her kidneys inexplicably started working again. Still, Elizabeth continues to suffer from kidney stones, including an episode that took place as recently as July 2008. However, Elizabeth Ellis has suffered from kidney stones for decades. This condition existed before the stroke, and likely will remain long after it.

She also paid a visit to Dr. Tomas Holmlund, a neurologist at the Dent Neurological Institute of Amherst and Orchard Park, to get some answers about what had happened to her. After looking at her MRI, he was astonished that she had lived. She apparently had suffered a "vena" stroke, accompanied by severe hemorrhaging in the brain.

All strokes fall into one of two categories. The first kind of stroke is known as "ischemic," typified by a blood clot in the brain. This is the most frequent, treatable, and survivable form of stroke. The second type, a vena (or vein) stroke is also known as "hemorrhagic." A hemorrhagic stroke starts when a vein or artery in the brain "leaks or bursts. This causes bleeding inside the brain or near the surface of the brain. Hemorrhagic strokes are less common but more deadly than ischemic strokes."[57] Mrs. Ellis had suffered the lethal hemorrhagic stroke.

*Author's personal collection*

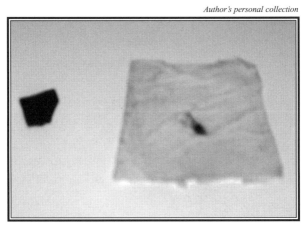

*The Baker rabbi that was placed on Elizabeth Ellis.*

Holmlund was stunned not only that she had survived, but that there was virtually no mental or physical impairment. The only thing in Elizabeth's case that can be pointed to is the pain and difficulty in moving her left leg and a bit slower mathematical processing. However, I should point out that in each case the function is there. It was restored. The quality of the function is not ideal, but it is there. The mathematical processing is possible. The left leg and the left foot do move. She was healed. She recovered. She lived.

And she is still improving. In 2006, Liz cut herself in a few places while shaving her left leg. This was particularly frightening news because she apparently does not have proper blood flow in that leg due to the stroke. The cuts did not heal for two years. She tried all kinds of creams and was about to seek further medical advice when the thought occurred to her to try something else. Why not use Baker's rabbi that had been placed on her body while she was in the coma? The cuts healed within three days.

In looking back at this story, it truly is one of the most impressive Baker-related narratives. The line of prayer and relics to Nelson Baker himself seems distinct and direct. The healing appears to be permanent and virtually complete, with exceptions only when looked at qualitatively, not quantitatively. What we are dealing with here is a case that might at least raise some eyebrows at the Vatican.

In final analysis though, this is not nearly as important to one man of faith.

"I will take her with a bad left foot any day," Tim Ellis said. "The point is that she is alive. That is the miracle. She was dead and Father Baker interceded. There is no doubt in my mind."

*Chapter Fourteen:*
# THE CHANCE ENCOUNTER?

Although it is only a two-page newsletter, the February 1989 edition of *Franciscan Gleanings* contained an impressive Father Baker story that has long since been forgotten. Considering the fact that the readership of this humble little circular amounted to no more than the Sisters of St. Francis, it is likely that few have ever heard of this event that happened when Baker was in his late 50s. It is an incident that brings to mind the seemingly unlimited power that this Lackawanna priest had at his disposal. We will see here, yet again, Baker perhaps crossing paths with that mysterious gift of bilocation.

This narrative comes to us from Sister Eileen Pinkel, O.S.F. With her further help, and the use of her article "Father Baker Remembered" from *Franciscan Gleanings*, we can now fully chronicle this fateful occurrence.[58]

Sister Eileen's connections to Father Baker come from two members of her family. Her father, Lawrence, was a salesman in the early 1900s, and he occasionally sold paint and supplies to Baker's institutions, likely meeting the OLV pastor on a few occasions. Sister Pinkel's sister, Loretto, was a long-time friend of a woman named Helen Sullivan. According to Sister Eileen, Helen and Loretto "were quite a team"[59] as an integral part of Buffalo's branch of the Ladies of Charity, a Catholic service organization dedicated to helping those in need. Through Loretto, Sister Pinkel also became good friends with Helen and liked to visit Miss Sullivan at the Holy Family Home in North Buffalo, especially as Helen grew older and less able to take care of herself. During a visit in 1989, Sullivan began talking about Father Baker, and an incident that happened the year that she was born - 1900. It was something that her mother told Helen about throughout her entire life until her mom died in 1937.

Helen's mother, Nell, worked for Baker at St. Patrick's Parish in some capacity. It is unclear exactly what she did, but she likely assisted in fundraising, and various works of charity. In addition to her responsibilities at the institutions, Nell was also a young mother. A worried young mother. Her little girl, Helen, had been born with "congenital torticollis."

*Torticollis, also known as 'wryneck,' (sic) is a condition in which (a) baby's head is tilted. The chin points to one shoulder, while the head tilts toward the opposite shoulder. Treatment is necessary to prevent (a) baby's face and skull from growing unevenly and to prevent limited motion of the head and neck. 'Congenital' means a condition that is present at birth. Congenital torticollis occurs when the neck muscle that runs up and toward the back of (the) neck is shortened.*[60]

This malady can only be treated by repetitive, daily physical therapy, or if that fails, corrective surgery. Both of these can of course be painful, ineffective, and costly. Perhaps with this in mind, Nell turned to a third possible solution, a miracle.

This young mother's thoughts turned not to Nelson Baker, but to the Saint Anne de Beaupre Shrine in Quebec. Perhaps out of humility she decided to avoid asking her employer for divine assistance, instead opting to plan a trip to Canada to visit this world-renowned pilgrimage site. This basilica dedicated to St. Anne, the mother of the Blessed Virgin Mary, is located in the village of Beaupre, approximately 25 miles northeast of Quebec City. In the 1650s, several shipwrecked sailors in the Gulf of St. Lawrence believed that they had been saved by the intercession of St. Anne. In thanksgiving, they decided to build a chapel in her honor at the nearby village of Beaupre.[61]

During construction of the church in 1658, the healing of a man by the name of Louis Guimond allegedly took place, said to be the first of countless other miracles that would follow. Through all of the various incarnations of the church, one element has remained constant - the healings. Through the centuries people have left crutches, canes, wheelchairs, and other artifacts at the shrine as evidence of their belief that St. Anne has interceded on their behalf. The healing power of the basilica is said to flow from the fountain in front of the church.

*Photo courtesy of Sister Eileen Pinkel, O.S.F.*

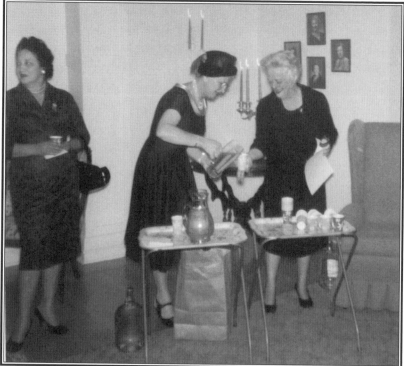

*Helen Sullivan, far right, before a Ladies of Charity board meeting in October 1962.*

About 1.5 million visitors make the journey to this shrine each year.[62] In the year 1900, Nell Sullivan wanted to be one of them. That is, until she heard her doorbell ring. It was Nelson Baker. She was frantically packing to leave, but did not want to be rude so she answered the door. This is how Sister Pinkel recounted the ensuing conversation as it was related to her by Helen Sullivan.

*"Oh, I'm sorry that I can't see you now," said Helen's mother, "as I'm on the way to catch a train."*

*"Where are you going?" Baker asked.*

*"We're taking the baby to St. Anne de Beaupre in hopes that we'll obtain a cure for her," was her response.*

*"Nell Sullivan!" Father Baker retorted, "with Our Lady of Victory in your backyard! Why are you taking that child to Quebec?"*

At this point, Sullivan instantly cancelled her plans and headed to St. Patrick's Parish to pray to Our Lady of Victory. According to Helen, she was "instantly" cured of her disease.

Three observations must be made at this point in the narrative. First, it would be out of character and quite unlikely if Father Baker did not accompany Nell Sullivan on her way back to the church to pray with her, and probably also over the baby. This would place him at the scene of the miracle and assign more "credit" to him for its apparent success.

Second, for this cure to be "instantaneous" makes some practical sense due to the type of condition that afflicted Helen. If her neck and head were askew, it would be quite evident to those witnessing this event if that condition suddenly corrected itself. These dramatic "all or nothing" type miracles are common with Baker. We saw in *The Mysteries of Father Baker* how he healed a girl confined to a wheelchair at the Blessed Sacrament Altar, or the nurse Miss Clark who was pronounced dead at Our Lady of Victory Hospital and then came back to life. The point to be made here is that "instantaneous" cures of something like cancer, for example, cannot be verified on the spot. Tests and analysis have to be done. An "instantaneous" cure of something like wry neck on the other hand, would be immediately evident to all witnesses.

Third, this is now the third time during the course of my research on Nelson Baker when there has been at least the suggestion that Baker may have been gifted with the ability to bilocate. The first two times were examined in *Mysteries*, during the Miss Clark episode, and as a result of a certain letter submitted to the *Victorian* magazine.[63]

Bilocation is the ability of a human being to appear in two places at the same time. One theory is that the soul leaves the body behind, and is then able to reappear in bodily form elsewhere, instantaneously. This is a gift known to only the most sacred and pious of human beings such as the Italian mystic Padre Pio. Part of the thinking on this matter is that a holy man or woman is so desperately needed somewhere else, but simply cannot get there in time. The body and the soul then separate to allow the individual to arrive at an exact place and time without having to physically travel that distance.

This episode with Nell Sullivan seems to suggest this. Sullivan was just about to leave her home in Lackawanna to catch a train to Canada. Just before she left, Baker showed up. Is this just a coincidence? How is it that he knew where to be at exactly the right moment? Was his physical body too far away to get to the Sullivan house in time? Did he somehow know that the child would not be healed in Quebec, and that he would instead be able to perform the healing? At the very least Baker has a habit of being where he is needed, when he is needed. Is this bilocation? Is it clairvoyance? Unfortunately such questions cannot be completely answered. We lack a record of a witness to state that he was in another place at the same time. Yet where there is smoke, there usually is fire. We have seen now three "puffs of smoke." We yearn for proof of that fire.

This would not be the last time that Baker and Helen Sullivan would cross paths. Sister Eileen recorded another short encounter between Baker and the Sullivan clan that transpired in 1907. "Helen herself was particularly fond of infants and prayed often that her mother would give her a baby sister or brother like her neighborhood companions had," wrote Sister Pinkel. Perhaps little Helen was offering up this request because all of her siblings, Irene, Albert, and Charles, were all older than her. Wouldn't it be nice to have a little baby brother or sister to play with?

One day, seven-year-old Helen was praying in the living room by the piano bench and said "Please God, give me a baby." Father Baker happened to be in the next room having a conversation with her mother when he heard the little voice in the next room. Nell explained that it was Helen. "She's always praying like that. I'll tell her to stop," she said to the St.

Patrick's pastor.

"No, let her be," Baker said. "Helen knows the right way to pray."

It was not long before Helen Sullivan had a little baby sister, Marie. Did Father Baker pray for Nell to be able to conceive another child? Perhaps. Consider that by 1907 Nell was no longer a young woman. She was 45 years old. Did he hear that little girl's prayers and then interceded on her behalf? Or is this just another coincidence?

*Photo courtesy of the Buffalo Catholic Diocese Archives*

*Father Baker laying the cornerstone at the Our Lady of Charity Refuge, 485 Best Street, Buffalo, a home for disadvantaged youth run by the Ladies of Charity.*

Father Baker was certainly a model for Helen Sullivan's life. "Incidents such as these could well have helped to shape Helen's future," wrote Sister Eileen, "for she eventually dedicated her life to caring for the homeless, the unwed mothers, infants, and other needy people from various walks of life," just like Father Baker. In 1932, she was appointed Program Director of Buffalo's branch of the Ladies of Charity. She held this position for 35 years.

The Ladies of Charity was formed in 1617 by Saint Vincent de Paul. The group first came to the United States in 1857 and by 1960 was organized under the Association of the Ladies of Charity of the United States. Women join this organization to give aid and assistance to all those in need. It is also an integrated part of the National Conference of Catholic Charities. Although much smaller in numbers now, throughout the 1900s Buffalo's branch of the Ladies of Charity operated, or helped to run, a number of homes for the aged, the chronically ill, and disadvantaged youth. These included the St. Vincent de Paul Health Camp at Angola-on-the-Lake, and the Our Lady of Charity Refuge on Best Street in Buffalo.[64]

Throughout her life, Helen Sullivan knew of all the names of the perhaps 2,000 or so members of the Ladies of Charity. This certainly came in handy at official gatherings with the bishop. Helen would stand behind the prelate and discretely whisper into his ear the names of all of the women as they came forward to shake his hand. These ladies walked away mildly shocked, but were most "awed and impressed" by this stunning display of mental acumen, according to Sister Eileen.

The absence of Helen Sullivan was certainly felt throughout the Buffalo Diocese when she passed away in June 1992. She was particularly missed by her dear friend, Loretto, Sister Pinkel's sister. During Helen Sullivan's Mass of Christian Burial, "my sister had the Ladies of Charity form a guard of honor inside Blessed Sacrament Church on Delaware Avenue in Buffalo," said Sister Eileen. "A fine tribute to a grand lady," and to a life shaped and protected in no small measure by the healing and guiding hands of Nelson Baker.

# *Chapter Fifteen:*
# THE CHAPEL APPARITION

As we noted above, Father Baker has been said to appear all throughout the Basilica, including the gift shop, the basement hallway, and on the main floor of the church. Perhaps the most distinctive aspect to this case, as we will see, is that it suggests that Baker's apparition may not be confined just to his beloved shrine.

Let us first mention the three sources for this event. The first is the subject of this incident, who wishes to remain anonymous. We will call her Bethany. The second is Bethany's brother, Vincent. The third is a friend of Bethany, "Anne," from the "Sacristy Miracle" chronicled above. We will simply combine the accumulated knowledge of these three sources, since none of the accounts conflict with the other versions. Each, however, was able to fill in holes that the other person could not. In no case did the sources contradict what the other sources said.[65]

Our story begins at Father Baker's funeral in 1936. Vincent remembers the affection that his parents, Kenneth and Blanche, shared for Father Baker. The couple made a point of waiting in line for hours to pay their last respects to the late OLV pastor. What further connection Kenneth and Blanche had to Baker is not known, but Bethany carried this devotion to Father Baker throughout her life. Although she is now a member of St. Ambrose Parish because of its more convenient location, she was at one time a long-serving member of Our Lady Victory Parish, even becoming acquainted with the late Pastor Robert C. Wurtz. Our Lady of Victory became a home for the family. Bethany's children were baptized and married there, and she made a point of bringing the family to witness Baker's reburial inside Our Lady of Victory Basilica in March 1999.

One place specifically that always seemed to offer comfort to her was the chapel at the now-closed Our Lady of Victory Hospital. The hospital was one of Baker's many achievements, opening up on October 2, 1919,[66] and was also of course the location where Father Baker passed away on July 29, 1936.

"She liked the private nature of the chapel," Vincent said. The site became a kind of refuge for her in the late 1970s. According to Anne, she was going through some hard times at this point in her life when she was in her late 30s. Bethany liked to bring her son with her to pray there and meditate.

The boy was only seven years old in 1978 when mother and son were walking in the hallway alongside the chapel at Our Lady of Victory Hospital and Father Baker apparently appeared to her. Her description of his apparition is consistent with the other ones of Baker that we have discussed. According to Bethany, Baker was wearing priestly vestments better suited for hundred years ago. He was cloaked in a black cassock trimmed in red with a large black hat. There was no doubt to her that it was Baker. He had a very "dusty appearance" and he looked like death itself. This of course was the same building where Baker died 42 years prior.

According to Bethany their conversation was brief. To this day she is unable to determine why he chose to appear to her. She was not praying to him at the time, but did many times after the apparition happened. One of the first things he said to her was "I suppose this hat looks funny," so he removed it. They then slowly walked together and talked for at least five minutes, before he suddenly disappeared from her side.

It is interesting to note that her son has no recollection of the apparition. This is not unusual. We noted in "The Healing Vision" and "The Peace Miracle" that in those cases Baker showed himself to only one person. One also has to wonder if Baker somehow disguised himself to others who may have spotted him. This might account for the five minutes that they were able to walk and talk along that hallway. It brings to mind Christ disguising

Himself after His resurrection, and only revealing His true identity after sometimes playfully conversing with His disciples.

There is one magnificent detail about this encounter with the dead that seems to confirm the authenticity of the incident. The strongest memory from this conversation that 68 year old Bethany retains to this day is that Father Baker told her that some day she would go to Medjugorje.

We detailed in "The Sacristy Miracle" that Medjugorje is a place in Bosnia-Herzegovina where many people believe that the Blessed Virgin Mary appeared and continues to appear to a faithful following. In fact, as Baker predicted, this woman did go to Medjugorje. Three times.

Critics might point out that this is a self-fulfilling prophecy. Perhaps, but you must also consider one immutable fact. In 1978, when Baker appeared to Bethany, the Marian apparitions at Medjugorje had not happened yet. They began in 1981. In 1978, there was no reason to go there, yet Baker somehow knew that his beloved Mary would be appearing in Bosnia three years into the future, and that this woman was going to go there.

Bethany is certain on this point, but it made no sense to her at the time. How could it? In 1978, except for in Bosnia, there wasn't a soul on this Earth who had even heard of that town. Indeed her pilgrimages there were profound spiritual journeys that deeply touched and changed her life. Yet equally impressive is Baker's ability to see into the future. He somehow had foreknowledge of perhaps the most controversial event in the Twentieth Century for the Catholic Church. Baker's connection to Mary seems to have only strengthened with death. The divine plans of heaven itself are at his disposal.

Truly what are the limits of this man's gifts?

*Chapter Sixteen:*
# BAKER'S FINAL EARTHLY MIRACLE?

The story has been handed down in the O'Connor family for generations, but not in the usual way. This particular tale was so important to the fabric of the men and women involved that it was written down, a step few people take when it comes to documenting and remembering family history.

The details of the narrative are well known to Mrs. Mary Lou O'Connor, having frequently heard them from her late mother, Mrs. Hortense Hawkins, one of the central players in this drama.[67] Hawkins decided to take her aging mother, Mrs. Mary Boland, to see the Our Lady of Victory Basilica in the early 1930s. Boland lived in Chicago, so Mrs. Hawkins felt that a trip to Our Lady of Victory would be a nice excursion during her visit to see the family.

A visit to the Basilica was not all that these ladies had in mind. They also wanted to see, and hopefully meet, Father Nelson Baker. Much to their delight Baker was at the Mass that they attended. Mary Lou O'Connor is not certain if Baker actually said the Mass. Considering his advanced age, he may have simply assisted, or watched. Either way, after the services concluded, the mother and daughter duo decided to wait for the OLV pastor outside of the church, before he made his way back to the rectory. Sure enough, along came Father Baker, accompanied by a young priest, Father Joseph M. McPherson. This single detail, the fact that Baker was walking with Father McPherson is of enormous importance. It is the key to the entire narrative and jumps out at us like a clue in a Sherlock Holmes saga.

The presence of Father McPherson allows us to pin this story down to a less than two month window of time. This young priest was ordained in 1936 and was quickly assigned to Our Lady of Victory as an assistant to the pastor. McPherson was a natural fit because he had grown up knowing all about the famous Lackawanna priest, hearing many stories from his brother-in-law, who had been like a father to him. McPherson's brother-in-law had sold furniture to the institutions for years and became quite friendly with Father Baker. Most likely when McPherson showed up for his assignment in June 1936, it was not the first time that he been to Our Lady of Victory, but it was the first time that he was there as a priest. He met Baker in Our Lady of Victory Hospital and gave Baker his blessing. Father McPherson would end up being the last assistant appointed to aid the aging OLV pastor, and likely the only one who Baker did not personally appoint.[68]

*Photo courtesy of Mrs. Mary Lou O'Connor*  *Photo courtesy of Mrs. Mary Lou O'Connor*

*Mrs. Mary Boland in the late 1920s. Did she receive Baker's final miracle on this Earth?*

*Mrs. Hortense Hawkins in 1936.*

Let us begin then to narrow down the time frame that the above encounter between the two ladies and the two priests could have taken place, so that we can understand the significance of it once we describe it later. We should note at the outset that Mary Boland placed this encounter in 1932. However, the presence of Father McPherson, especially that he was "Father" McPherson (ordained in 1936), seems to rule that out. In her own notes on the encounter, Mary Boland said "Fr. McPherson was standing beside him (Father Baker) and so was I." Biographer Floyd Anderson wrote that this newly ordained priest arrived at OLV in June 1936. If we allow for the earliest possible date in June for McPherson's appearance, we can obviously then place him at the parish no earlier than June 1, 1936. Baker died on July 29, 1936. The dying pastor received the Last Rites on July 17. This likely means that Baker never left his room after July 17 until he died 12 days later.

Anderson also noted that the 94 year-old prelate had started to decline in the spring of that year. "(H)is health and memory had been quite poor," he wrote in his 1960 biography. "He had started to slip noticeably in April, both physically and mentally; and from then on, except for the occasional 'good' days, his health deteriorated."[69]

Therefore using the above information, the encounter in question must have taken place between June 1 and July 17, 1936, during one of Baker's "good" days. Considering that Baker was already hospitalized when McPherson arrived, this may have been the last time that the OLV pastor was even able to walk on his own power, much less outside on the parish grounds. I feel safe in concluding that this was likely the final miracle that Father Nelson Baker performed on this earth. It does not seem possible that time or circumstances could have allowed for any other miracles during the last days of his life. Even by July 12, he was too weak to read or even sign some paperwork.[70]

Let us then proceed to describe this fateful encounter. If you can picture the scene, imagine a frail, hundred-pound, hunched-over, five foot-four priest slowly making his way out of Our Lady of Victory Basilica with his youthful, nervous assistant inching along his side, likely praying that the old man would not fall, perhaps questioning why he even allowed him out his hospital bed. Nelson Baker may have known instinctively that he was needed one more time. One last time.

During his near century of life he had likely conjured up the power to cure the diseased, calm a storm, find gas wells, bilocate, and literally raise the dead. Could his aging hands, could his crippled body, could his fading memory, still summon the power of God one final time on this earth to heal another human being? That is exactly what Mrs. Hortense Hawkins humbly found herself asking this man.

Hawkins explained that her mother, Mary, was not doing well. It is likely at this point that Baker at least perked up a bit upon hearing that sacred name. The younger woman explained that her elderly mother was suffering from "hardening of the arteries," a polite term for what is now called Alzheimer's Disease. Years ago, when a person suffered from this mysterious ailment, it was assumed that the arteries in the brain had hardened, causing a deterioration in mental functions. Mary Boland was very weak physically, was often confused, and was suffering from advanced memory loss.

"Will you please bless her Father?" Hawkins humbly asked Baker. The aging mystic then spoke only two words. Perhaps that was all that he could. "Kneel down," he said, looking at Mary Boland. She then knelt in front of him as he extended his hands over the old woman's head, and blessed her, and her daughter.

After he was finished, Boland returned to her feet and watched as Father Baker began to fumble with his vestments. He removed a pin from his own clothing that bore the image of his beloved Our Lady of Victory. Father Baker then pinned this medal directly onto Boland. After this final gesture, Baker likely just continued on his way, walking slowly with Father McPherson toward the rectory. The OLV pastor typically behaved in this self-effacing way after allegedly performing a miracle, always quickly and quietly exiting the scene, never seeking notoriety, already on to the next task.

As for Mary Boland, her daughter Hortense could not get over how instantly improved her mother was. All during the car ride home, Mary could not stop chatting. She seemed like her old self again. Her memory was back, and gone was that embarrassing confusion. For the next nine months until her death, Boland enjoyed complete mental clarity, and lived out her final months in good health. She died on Saturday, March 13, 1937. Importantly, Boland did not die of physical or mental ailments. She suffered a horrible fall during which she hit her skull violently. She never recovered. Absent this tragic accident, she would likely have lived many years longer in her persistent good health. She was 73 years old. During those months after she met Father Baker, Boland kept the Our Lady of Victory medal with her constantly.

This apparent miracle yet again provides us with an example of the potent mix of suffering with piety that can lead to the miraculous. In this case, Baker could easily empathize with what Mary Boland was going through. Baker himself was suffering from the same ailments at that time, including memory loss, and poor physical health. We have here yet again an indication that the miraculous may be a profound pious, spiritual empathy, the miraculous code that we seek to understand.

*Author's personal collection*

*Baker's Our Lady of Victory medal that he pinned to the clothing of Mrs. Mary Boland. Was this the relic that he performed his final Earthly miracle with?*

This story is also quite fitting for Baker's last earthly dip into the supernatural. Here he is on death's door, unwilling to stay confined to his bed, still helping people, still refusing to seek any accolades for his miraculous work. It is also stunning to consider the ease with which he could summon the divine power to heal another human being. His physical body was nearly crippled, but it seemed to make little difference to him. At that stage in his life, such a healing like this was probably second nature to him.

As we will see later in our discussion of the Gauchat and Metz relic collections, Baker was also strangely giving away nearly all of his earthly possessions in the last weeks and months of his life. He no doubt knew that his days were numbered and perhaps sought to sever all earthly ties to material possessions in an attempt to purify his soul for death. The gift of his own medal of Our Lady of Victory that he likely pinned to his clothing every day as a badge of honor, is consistent with this larger pattern of giving away items as we will see later.

The pin (2CR) itself is now in the possession of Mary Lou O'Connor. It is a remarkable item. On the front is the traditional representation of the Blessed Virgin Mary under her title of Our Lady of Victory, that of her holding the infant Jesus in her right arm. Christ is also standing on the earth. As we will examine in Chapter Three during our discussion of the Gauchat and Metz relics, this comforting, maternal pose was Baker's preferred image of his closest confidant. He favored this motherly image above all others. In fact, the O'Connor medal is essentially a miniature version of his most prized earthly possession, as we detail in the next chapter. On the back of the medal is a capital "M" topped off with a cross.

As for that newly ordained priest, he went on to become superintendent at Our Lady of Victory, and later would vouch for the veracity of this miraculous tale. Mrs. Hawkins was insistent on this point, and was not shy in telling anyone who would ask (and some perhaps who didn't) "You can go ask Father McPherson if this didn't happen."

*Father Baker in the 1920s.*

# PART THREE: SECRETS OF THE GAUCHAT/METZ RELICS

*Chapter Seventeen:*
# THE MICHAEL GAUCHAT COLLECTION: BAKER'S "HOLY GRAIL?"

I had the honor of speaking about Father Baker to a group of people at the Hamburg Public Library on a hot spring night in 2005. After I had finished my presentation, an elderly gentleman raised his hand and told the assembled crowd that he had the good fortune of meeting Nelson Baker when he was a little boy, even getting the chance to receive a blessing from the aging pastor, and shake his hand. "I'll only charge a dollar each to anyone who wants to touch my hand after the lecture," he announced to roaring laughter.

All good humor has an element of truth to it. Such a story serves to bring up a larger question about Baker. Was this man so powerful that even the things that he touched became infected with his supernatural power? The answer to that question appears to be yes. We have documented several cases in this book and in *Mysteries* (such as the use of his cross) that seem to prove the effectiveness of using Baker artifacts.

One curious phenomenon that reflects this is that an unknown number of people in Western New York continue to have in their possession countless relics of Nelson Baker, more than 70 years after his death. These items include pieces of his clothing, medals he blessed, dirt from his original grave, statues, candles, crosses, and even locks of his hair.

One difficult aspect in researching these items is proving that they actually came from the OLV pastor. There are essentially two rules to use to determine if an artifact came from Nelson Baker. First, is the item in question something that Baker might reasonably have used, or blessed? For example, an allegedly Baker-blessed chia pet, or rubix cube might be safely dubbed slightly anachronistic. Second, is there a clear line of documentation that can trace the item back to Nelson Baker?

Another issue would be the age of the relic. Is the artifact at least about 70 years old? This I hesitate to make a rule because appearances can be deceiving. Many people preserve these items and take meticulous care of them so that they often appear quite new. Admittedly, these general guidelines are all hard, if not impossible, to substantiate. In the final analysis, the character and honesty of the men and women who possess these pieces of the past are the most important factors to rely upon.

*Author's personal collection*

*Incense burner. Relic one of five.*

In this section we will examine the Father Baker relic collections of Michael Gauchat and Joseph Metz. Together, these men independently possess two of the most impressive sets of Baker artifacts that exist outside of the Father Baker Museum in the basement of Our Lady of Victory Basilica. The most remarkable aspect of these Baker pieces is that they easily satisfy all of the above criteria. As we will see, the items all appear to be the type of things that Baker could have made use of, there is a clear line of documentation that indicates that Baker once owned the items, and the integrity of the men involved is beyond question. Neither Gauchat nor Metz seeks any notoriety or monetary gain from their possession of the relics. Let us begin with the collection of Michael Gauchat.[71]

The Gauchat clan has always had a deep respect for the Lackawanna humanitarian, even passing down from generation to generation the threat of "being sent to Father Baker's" for misbehaving. On one trip to Baker's original grave in Holy Cross Cemetery, Gauchat's young daughter, Heather, stomped her foot on the burial plot, boldly insisting "You stay in there Father Baker!"

*Author's personal collection*

*Our Lady of Victory pergola. Relic two of five.*

It is not just idle warnings that have been handed down in the Gauchat family, but also a superlative set of Baker artifacts. Let us then trace the line back to Nelson Baker. Michael Gauchat received five (nine if counted separately) Baker items from his uncle, John F. Welch, on October 22, 1999. Why would Welch give these items to his nephew? There are several reasons. The men share a close bond. Gauchat's own father died at the age of 46, and as Welch reached his elderly years, he wanted these items to be safely in the hands of someone he loved and trusted. Welch knew that his nephew is a deeply religious man. Not only does he have a respect for Father Baker, Gauchat is a Third Order Franciscan.

Followers of St. Francis of Assisi fall into three groups. The first order consists of ordained brothers and priests. The second order is made up of nuns. The third order has lay men and women who lead secular lives, but maintain a religious devotion to the Franciscan way of life. In short, Michael Gauchat seemed a natural fit for a caretaker of these special items. In fact, he protects and honors them with a knight-like devotion, cradling them like the care given to a newborn, displaying them with respect in his home.

The next question would logically be, "how did John F. Welch obtain this collection?" Looking for some work in the spring of 1940, Welch taught some wayward youth at a Father Baker camp in East Eden. These boys had been arrested by the police and were sent to this reform camp to "straighten out." Welch taught them to read, write, and do some basic math. While working at the camp, Welch lived on the third floor of the Our Lady of Victory Protectory, most likely doing some occasional maintenance work there. He soon struck up a friendship with some of the Brothers of the Holy Infancy, who also lived on the grounds, and had worked with Nelson Baker. He became quite close with one in particular – Brother Thomas. This man was Father Baker's valet, driving the aging pastor to various events around the diocese in the final years of his life. On July 10, 1940, Brother Thomas gave these relics to John F. Welch. Getting on in years himself, and seeking a caretaker for the items, the good brother "wanted to do for me what Father Baker had done for him,"

Welch recalled in 2008. Perhaps the gifts were a reward for Welch's service to the boys that Nelson Baker so loved and cherished.

*Crucifix with two candleholders and one candle. Relic three of five.*

The final question remains, "how and why did Brother Thomas receive these artifacts?" According to John F. Welch and Michael Gauchat, Brother Thomas received these items directly from Nelson Baker as a gift shortly before his death in 1936. The exact circumstances of when, how, and why these items were bequeathed to Brother Thomas are not known and may never be known. However, we can make an informed guess at the very least as to why. To speculate on this, we first need to explain in detail what the Gauchat collection consists of.

Stated simply, the pieces appear to be a traveling mass set, with one important addition. Together, they would be nearly everything that Baker might need to perform a small, private mass as he often did at convents, chapels, and even homes. The first item is an incense burner (2CR) that actually separates into two pieces. The second piece is a small statue of Our Lady of Victory (2CR) standing inside of a pergola. The third artifact is actually four individual items: a standing crucifix (2CR), two candle holders (2CR), and one candle (2CR). (The other candle is missing.)

The fourth relic is a priestly vestment (2CR) that ties around the neck and falls onto the chest like a bib. It is known as a "rabbi." A rabbi is defined as "a short breastpiece of cloth or silk fitted to a Roman collar; a rabat. In the Roman Catholic Church, the rabbi of priests is black, of prelates purple, or cardinals red."[72] This particular rabbi has vine-like embroidering, appears to be silk, and is purple or perhaps fuchsia in color, perfectly fitting the definition. A "prelate" is defined as "an ecclesiastic of superior rank and authority, a dignitary of the church…They wear a distinctive costume and enjoy, especially in the higher ranks, special liturgical or ceremonial privileges."[73] Baker was named a "domestic prelate, with the title of Right Reverend Monsignor, by Pope St. Pius X in 1905, and Prothonotary Apostolic by Pope Pius XI in 1922."[74]

In other words, the fact that this is a purple rabbi makes complete sense. Baker would definitely wear this color as a prelate of distinction in the Buffalo Diocese. If the rabbi was black, it could raise questions as to its authenticity because they are more common among priests. Certainly a black rabbi could date from Baker's early days, but because the rabbi is purple, this color serves to further confirm its genuineness since so few priests reach the rank of prelate, and are allowed to wear that color.

The final item is the most important of the set. It is a partially damaged (and repaired) statue of Our Lady of Victory (2CR) holding the infant Jesus. As we mentioned above in "Baker's Final Earthly Miracle?," this is the traditional depiction of the Blessed Virgin Mary under her title of Our Lady of Victory. Christ is standing on the Earth. The statue is about the length of an average adult's arm. This statue is very famous in Baker-lore. It was quite simply Nelson Baker's most prized Earthly possession. I am quite certain that many people have wondered where it has been all of these years. To explain its importance it is worth quoting biographer Floyd Anderson at some length.

*When he went on a trip, the statue was the last item packed into his bag*
*and the first one out of it. He would put it on the dresser in his room,*
*wherever he might be, and then he was at home again. As he grew older,*
*it seemed that he wanted the statue of Our Lady of Victory with him all*
*the time. Even when he went to bed at night, he would cradle it in his*
*arm as he fell asleep, just as a child might do with a favorite toy.*[75]

According to Anderson, Baker even took the statue with him into the
surgery room at Our Lady of Victory Hospital when he had his right eye
removed in December 1927. "The statue was cradled in his arms there, too,
until the anesthetic made him unconscious, and when his arms relaxed the
statue toppled to the floor." Worried about his reaction, the hospital atten-
dants rushed the statue back to the Protectory to have it repaired by a
Brother of the Holy Infancy whom Anderson did not identify. It is possible
that the brother in question was in fact Brother Thomas. In any case, the
statue was restored, and returned to its owner after the successful surgery.[76]

To be sure, the statue in the Gauchat collection is damaged and obviously
has been repaired, especially around the head of Our Lady of Victory and
the right arm of the infant Christ, which may have hit the floor first if Baker
was cradling it in his right arm.

Now having explained in detail all of the items in the collection, we
must make the link between Brother Thomas and Father Baker. Brother
Thomas was Nelson Baker's valet, although doubtless the humble OLV
pastor would scoff at such a term. As Baker got older and his eyesight got
worse, he needed someone to take him to the various sites that he went to,
be they boat trips, Masses, business events, the local jail, or even the Baker
farms on Martin Road. His mobility was becoming increasingly limited.
Keep in mind the fact that Baker had been walking with a limp since his
early 30s (from the effects of erysipelas) and one can appreciate the progressively debilitating effects of old age, and the resulting frustration to
such a fiercely independent man.

Brother Thomas would be uniquely positioned to know what Baker carried with him, and what items meant the most to him. When Baker traveled

away from Our Lady of Victory to say Mass, this traveling Mass kit would go with him. Not only that, Brother Thomas would almost certainly have assisted at these Masses, and even set up these pieces on a makeshift altar. In fact, it was on the way to a Mass at Mount Saint Joseph in Buffalo in December 1927 that Baker first complained to Brother Thomas of having pain in his right eye.[77] Brother Thomas was the one who insisted that his intense throbbing be checked by a doctor. This of course led to Baker having surgery to remove the eye, during which his prized statue broke.

*Author's personal collection*

*Rabbi. Relic four of five.*

The statue subsequently became intrinsically linked with the surgery because it was broken during it. Perhaps Baker recognized the role Brother Thomas had played in likely saving his life by insisting on seeing a doctor, and the statue was presented as a gift of thanks. It is also possible that someone else gave the statue to Brother Thomas after Baker died, perhaps linking him to the surgery and thus the statue. However, Gauchat and Welch insist that Baker gave the statue and the other items directly to Brother Thomas while Baker was still alive. They are adamant on this point. It does seem to make the most sense that Baker would see Brother Thomas as the best care-taker for these items. Brother Thomas would know more than anyone how special these items were to the aging prelate. He would have seen Baker holding them, cradling them, packing them, and unpacking them. The stat-ue would always have accompanied the traveling mass set. Baker took it everywhere, perhaps even secretly. Only Brother Thomas would truly have known how often he was attached to that statue. Only Brother Thomas would have set hands on the Mass set to help the aged hands of Father Baker perform Mass. There is no better candidate for these relics than Brother Thomas. In fact, if they ended up in the possession of someone else, it would raise suspicion.

Having then made the link, a few final points need to be made. First, what does this gift say about Father Baker? Let us be clear in pointing out just how significant a find this statue is. Many people who admire Baker and the work that he did have doubtless wondered what happened to this famous statue. It is the Holy Grail of Father Baker relics. It was quite sim-ply his most prized material possession. Nothing was dearer to him in his earthly life. It seemed to be a physical manifestation, a reminder of his beloved Our Lady of Victory. The two were inseparable. Such a gift to Brother Thomas speaks to the boundless charity, and pure altruism of this man. To part with such an item would not have been easy for him, but it was a choice that he made nonetheless.

Second, this gift may point to yet another power of Nelson Baker, clair-voyance. Baker likely knew through his near limitless gifts that his days on this earth were coming to a close, and therefore it was time to part with his worldly possessions. Such a gesture was just another sacrifice, another form of suffering to prepare and purify his body for death.

Perhaps even the realization that many of his goods would end up in a museum scared and repulsed this extremely humble man. Better to have a trusted friend have these sacred items than to have them confined behind

*Arm-length Our Lady of Victory statue. Relic five of five.*

glass. Michael Gauchat, selflessly seeking to share the statue with the public, even offered to have the Our Lady of Victory statue placed in the Baker museum at the Basilica, but Pastor Robert Wurtz declined the offer, instead telling Gauchat to "cherish it."

Certainly Michael Gauchat has indeed cherished these items, calling them "priceless." He also noted that to the best of his knowledge, none of the pieces have ever been used in an attempt to heal someone. One has to wonder what slumbering power may be lurking within these hallowed artifacts. Perhaps one day we will find out.

*Chapter Eighteen:*
# THE JOSEPH METZ COLLECTION:
# GLIMPSING BAKER'S PRIVATE LIFE

To meet Dan Metz is to be instantly overtaken by his gregarious, generous, good-natured demeanor. Always helpful and informative, Metz speaks lovingly about his elderly father, Joseph. The two share a special bond, even as they struggle to cope with Joseph's severe hearing loss. Dan fondly recalls the picnics and parties of his childhood with his father proudly using his new home movie camera, complete with its blinding set of lights.[78]

Just as precious as these memories are to Dan is a collection of Father Baker artifacts that have now passed into the hands of his father. Let us then trace the line of these items back to Nelson Baker, and see what we can cull from them in the process.

Joseph Metz became the owner of several different Baker relics on December 24, 2007, when his wife, Mary E. Metz, passed away. Mary had received these articles from the key figure in this narrative, Sister Blanche Don Pierre. Sister Blanche was a French Canadian nun who was a private assistant/caretaker/nurse for Nelson Baker in the final, physically declining years of his life. More importantly, Sister Don Pierre was also the sister of Joseph Metz's mother, in other words, his aunt. Sister Blanche had always taken a liking to the wife of her nephew. Dan recalls that his mother was kind of "like a daughter" to the French Canadian sister, who obviously had no children of her own. Being from South Buffalo, Mary also knew about Father Baker, and was quite involved in the Church, more so than any other member of the family. It seemed a natural fit then that shortly before she passed away, Sister Blanche gave her precious Baker relics to her beloved Mary.

*Photo courtesy of the Metz family*

*Sister Blanche Don Pierre, Father Baker's private assistant during the final years of his life.*

How then did Sister Blanche obtain these items? According to Joseph, Daniel, and most importantly Mary Metz, Sister Blanche said that the relics were a gift from Father Baker. To explain and better understand why Nelson Baker would give these articles to his caretaker, let us first detail what these items are.

The first artifact is a four piece tea strainer (2CR) that is immaculately preserved. The drinking cup portion of the set is strikingly deep blue, the color of the Blessed Virgin Mary, which may have attracted Baker to it. It was made in Germany and may have been purchased during Baker's trip to Europe as a seminarian. The amount of tea that would collect in the drinking cup is quite minimal and likely could be consumed in one or two sips, further proof of how little sustenance Baker consumed (or needed to consume) during his long life. The fine condition of the pieces seems to indicate that Baker likely took good care of this item, perhaps relying upon it for a short tea break during times of stress. His hands likely gripped this tea set during some of his darkest hours at the parish.

*Author's personal collection*

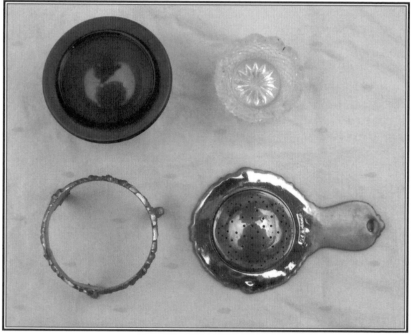

*Baker's personal tea brewing set.*

The second item is a small, grayish colored statue of Our Lady of Victory (2CR). The Metz family said Sister Blanche often saw this statue on Baker's dresser in his living quarters. Baker did not always sleep in his own bed. He would often give up his room if there were no more beds for the boys, or would collapse in prayer at the altar inside St. Patrick's Church, or Our Lady of Victory Basilica. But on the nights when he did turn in, this four inch statue would have been one of the first things that he would see in the morning, or one of the first things that his visitors would see in the morning.

There is one other essential point to make about this tiny little statue. Why would Baker bother with such a small item? We noted earlier Baker's childlike affection for his much larger statue of Our Lady of Victory, carrying it into surgery and even sleeping with it. Obviously, Baker could not carry that statue with him at all times, such as when performing mass, or meeting with business people. This smaller statue may have served as a stand–in for the larger one. It is an exact duplicate of the larger statue that we chronicled above. Our Lady of Victory is holding the infant Jesus in her right arm. Even the expressions are the same. It is also extremely worn. His fingers seem to have caressed it over and over again, perhaps surreptitiously in his pocket. It seems unlikely to be so weathered if it just sat on his dresser. This may have been his constant reminder of Our Lady of Victory. Perhaps he took this with him during the day, placed it on the dresser at night, and of course cradled the larger statue while sleeping. If this is the case, I would not hesitate to offer up this tiny little item as a good candidate for the second most prized earthly possession of Nelson Baker. This one may have done the grunt work with him, day in and day out.

Next on the list is a purple colored bag belonging to Sister Blanche that contains two items. The first is a little circular canister that is approximately one inch wide. At one time it may have held jewelry, or medicine. Inside however is a little piece of paper marked (in typed letters) "Father Baker Hair & Mantella." Sure enough, a short piece of hair (1CR) sits snugly inside the paper as does a reddish colored swatch of material (2CR). This cloth is actually protected by two pieces of paper that have been stitched together to seal the "mantella" inside. Most likely Sister Blanche typed these words herself and stitched the paper together to protect the fabric.

She seems to have been slightly mistaken in her spelling. The so-called "mantella" is most likely a "mantelletta" defined as "a short mantle of silk or wool with armholes, but without sleeves worn over the rochet by cardinals, bishops, and prelates of the first rank."[79] We noted above Baker's high rank as a prelate, so this identification as a mantelletta (allowing for the slight difference in wording) makes perfect sense that the textile would in fact be Baker's. It is a highly important piece of clothing that only the highest ranking priests, like Baker, were allowed to wear. It is the type of clothing that Baker certainly wore during the last years of his life when Sister Blanche was taking care of him. (For example, an elderly Baker can be seen wearing a mantelletta in the photo on the cover of *The Mysteries of Father Baker.*) It would make complete sense then that she would have access to this type of Baker vestment. The second item in the bag appears to be more of the same, another small piece of reddish mantelletta (2CR), and perhaps 50 strands of hair (1CR) that are also presumably Father Baker's. These items were placed between two pieces of plastic, and then stitched together by Sister Don Pierre.

The first two items, the tea set, and the OLV statue should be linked together as gifts directly from Baker. I think it is unlikely that the last two relics, the pieces of mantelletta, and the strands of hair, were gifts from Father Baker. Instead, they were most likely "privately obtained" by Sister Blanche at a convenient time. There were countless requests for relics of Baker during the last years of his life as his pious reputation increased. Baker would have none of this, rejecting any attempt to make himself into some kind of a living saint or cult figure. Nevertheless, Baker was powerless to prevent the nuns from secretly cutting up his clothes, or saving his hair without his knowledge. They knew that they were living with and working for a gifted mystic, and likely future saint. To save this man's hair and clothing was a sign of respect for him. And as one of Baker's private nurses, it would make perfect sense that Sister Don Pierre would have access to some of Baker's hair. Father Baker was certainly too frugal or too weak to go to the nearest Lackawanna barber. Instead, if his hair need trimming, the nuns could do just as good of a job with the little hair that he had left. It would have been during one of these haircuts that the good sister would have refused to discard his hair and instead saved and cherished it.

The tea set and the statue would also be items that she would have seen many times and even touched. She most likely prepared his tea, and even placed the little OLV statue in his clothing to begin his day. Perhaps only she would know the importance of the statue and the tea set. Only she would know what the items meant to him, or what stories accompanied their purchases.

*Author's personal collection*

*Left to right: Sister Blanche's carrying pouch, an encased piece of Baker's mantelletta with his several strands of his hair, and a pill box with another piece of Baker's hair and mantelletta enclosed inside.*

Let us think again of Baker's selflessness, of the certain knowledge of his impending death. It seems as if Baker wanted to leave this world without a single earthly possession, nothing to tie him here. Baker's will confirms this. In it he states:

> *I have no money in any bank, no bonds nor securities of any kind or form; and I am indebted to no one financially, and no one is indebted to me...I have no property of any kind, except certain chattels donated to me by kind friends during my life, such as books, altar furniture, certain articles of furniture, clothing, etc; and I wish the institutions which have been under my charge in Lackawanna, hereinafter named to have these.[80]*

The gift of the tea set and the statue are more examples of Baker choosing the route of self-sacrifice, of suffering. If this statue was indeed his second most prized possession on this earth, as logic dictates, parting ways with it would have been extremely difficult - like with the larger one mentioned in the Gauchat collection. And just like with that collection, to the best knowledge of the Metz family, these pieces of the past have never been used in an attempt to heal someone. And that may be the most striking feature about these two relic collections. To be frank, if any artifacts would seem to have the greatest likelihood of being employed for the miraculous, it would be these, and yet these families have never done so.

*Author's personal collection*

*Baker's pocket-sized statue of Our Lady of Victory.*

I think this fact alone speaks to the respect that the Gauchat family and the Metz family have for Nelson Baker. They seek nothing from him. They are not keeping these relics in some warped desire to tap into divine power.

If ever used, they no doubt would be employed with utmost respect, and only after careful consideration. Instead, the relics serve as a reminder of Baker's charity, innocence, frugality, and power to affect people generations after his death. Michael Gauchat, Joseph Metz, and whoever follows in their footsteps as caretakers of these sacred items, have become knights with the self-appointed task of handing down this legacy for future generations.

May their power never fade.

*Father Baker in 1925.*

# PART FOUR:
# UNLOCKING THE VATICAN

*Chapter Nineteen:*
# THE JOURNEY TO SAINTHOOD

One of the longest running jokes among those familiar with how the Catholic Church selects its candidates for sainthood is that somewhere deep within the Vatican walls they are still processing an application for Christopher Columbus. Although that pointless exercise was doubtless abandoned long ago, the yarn does hint at a larger truth. The Church is noto-riously slow when it comes to the saint-making business. In our fast-paced world, it is difficult to understand that the Vatican moves not in terms of days and weeks, but instead in decades and centuries. The process for the canon-ization of Nelson Baker, begun in the late 1980s, is therefore comparatively recent. Nevertheless, Baker has already completed the first of three steps to reach sainthood. I think it is useful as we move into the 21st Century to look at this process in some detail, and pause to point out the obstacles and advantages we can generally expect to encounter, as well as some unique circumstances that may serve to help or harm Baker's cause.

A useful place to begin is with a brief overview of the process itself.[81] First, five years must pass after the death of the candidate before any action can be taken. In the early days of the Church, saints were named by simple public acclamation among the people in the local diocese of a candidate. There has been a quiet movement among some Vatican leaders to return to this ancient format, especially for such iconic figures as Pope John Paul II, or Mother Theresa.

Second, the bishop of the diocese of the candidate in question must begin the investigation by forming a diocesan tribunal to investigate the person's life. Witnesses are called who can prove that the candidate exhibited virtues such as faith, hope, charity, prudence, justice, temperance, and fortitude. The Congregation for the Causes of Saints reviews the evidence to determine if the person lived a heroic life. Once this is demonstrated to the satisfaction of the committee, and the pope, the person is given the title "Servant of God" and may be referred to as "Venerable." Nelson Baker was awarded these distinctions in 1987, thus completing step one of three. Now the hard part.

The next stage is proof of a miracle attributed to the intercession of the candidate after his or her death. What is also required to complete this second stage is the submission of a "positio." This book-length document is essentially a type of selective biography of the candidate's life. It includes documents and arguments put together by the local diocese that are designed to prove the heroic virtue of the person. Baker's positio was submitted in 2001. If the positio is approved by the Vatican, and a posthumous miracle is verified by a team of investigators beyond all scientific doubt, the Holy Father will then grant the individual the title "Blessed." This intermediary phase, also known as "beatification," can last sometimes for centuries because of the requirement to fulfill the final obstacle, yet another miracle. And not just any miracle. This one must occur after the person was beatified, not just sometime after death, thus eliminating any potential miraculous stories that had taken place up to that point in time. Once completed, the Blessed attains the title "Saint." Canonization then assures public worship in the entire Church for this exulted man or woman.

With two posthumous miracles required for canonization, it is no wonder that countless promising prospects never make it to the end. A reasonable person might ask, "Why must the miracles be after death? Why does the Vatican not use miracles performed during the lifetime of the candidate?" In fact, if that were the case, it would seem that Baker might already be canonized, considering the portfolio of wonders that he apparently worked during his lifetime.

The answer is actually quite simple and involves a bit of theology and practicality. First, what is a saint? When the Catholic Church declares someone a saint, all they are saying is that the person is in heaven, in the presence of God. Posthumous miracles prove this. A candidate simply could not perform a miracle after death unless he or she was in the presence of God. Even after death, it's all about who you know. Second, posthumous miracles are more recent than miracles performed during a person's life, and are thus more easily investigated. There are many Blessed candidates from centuries ago whose miracles are virtually impossible to prove. But if a miracle crops up now, witnesses are still alive to prove or discount the event in question.

In fact, the process of investigation to prove a posthumous miracle can be quite rigorous. We have noted earlier some of the painstaking stipulations such as theological clarity. There must be no question as to who interceded on a person's behalf, such as with the ECMC coma miracle. In other words, Father Baker must be the only one a person or a family directed their prayers toward. Another aspect to the investigation process is to seek out miracles that are 100 percent in nature, such as complete healings or recoveries. This was the issue that disqualified Nelson Baker's undecomposed blood, mentioned previously. A certain permanence to the miracle is also considered necessary for eligibility. This is often what slows down the entire process. Even if a legitimate miracle is reported with clear theological clarity, complete healing, and good documentation, the Vatican will wait sometimes for years to see if the allegedly divine cure is permanent, and not a temporary phase easily explained away by science.

With a multitude of rules and regulations it is no wonder why many promising stories reported as "miracles" are quickly disqualified, and why so many causes for sainthood have failed, as people simply give up in the face of this bureaucratic Leviathan. Take the case of Joseph Donahue, for example. We briefly discussed his remarkable story in *The Mysteries of Father Baker*, but have recently learned more about the circumstances surrounding his illness and unexpected recovery.[82] More importantly for our purposes, the Donahue story will provide for us a prime example of those two essential ingredients in an official Vatican miracle: 100 percent healing, and permanence of recovery.

Just to briefly recap the main elements of the Donahue saga, 16-year-old Joseph Donahue was stricken with bacterial meningitis in August 2000. He was taken to Buffalo Children's Hospital where he immediately began to deteriorate. His eyes bled, his internal organs shut down, his heart stopped several times, and, mostly interestingly, his dead skin began peeling off his body. The flesh was excruciatingly painful to the touch, leaving scars all over his body. This last detail immediately catches our attention. We can now add this case to the long list of miracles associated with Father Nelson Baker that are skin-related. We noted in the biography section the connection between suffering and the miraculous, particularly the skin and eye suffering endured by Baker at the beginning and end of his priesthood. Baker endured months of intense pain due to the skin disease erysipelas, coping with the agony of pussing lesions all over his body. The wealth of skin-related Baker miracles, including perhaps this one, during his life and after his death, are undeniable.

The Baker connections in the Donahue case are extensive, including dirt used from Baker's original grave (3CR), rosary beads he had prayed with (2CR), and a piece of cloth from a vestment the OLV pastor had worn (2CR). Not only that, Donahue's uncle, a Catholic priest from Most Precious Blood Church in Buffalo, instructed the family to pray exclusively to Father Baker. At the very least then, here was a case with unquestioned theological clarity. The only person invoked for help was Nelson Baker.

Nevertheless, doctors gave this young man no chance for recovery and he was given the Last Rites. Death seemed certain as the teen sank further into the illness. However, after coming out of a ten-day medically induced coma, during which Baker's intercession was constantly invoked, Donahue began to unexpectedly recover. Through medication and constant therapy, he was able to return home on October 8, 2000. Although his kidneys functioned at only 25 percent, and he had lost a toe on his left foot, and half-a-toe on his right, the young man looked forward to a normal life. His skin had healed and he eventually was even taken off dialysis. Given the fact that Donahue had even dreamed about Father Baker during his comatose period, this seemed like the perfect miracle to move Baker up the path toward sainthood.

Those hopes were soon dashed.

We can clearly see that the teen was not completely healed. He lost one and a half toes, and never regained full function of his kidneys. In other words, the healing was not 100 percent in nature, as is required for consideration as an official miracle. But if Father Baker truly did intercede here to save the life of this young man, which the family firmly believes, then why did he not heal Donahue completely? There really is no clear answer to this question other than to point out how little we know about the realm of the miraculous, and the divine intentions that are likely at play here and beyond our understanding. Certainly during Baker's life, he did not heal every person in need of a miracle, often telling certain suffering individuals who would never recover that God's will would be done. Others he seemed to heal with the wave of his hand. Why the discrimination? Was he, for lack of a better phrase, following orders? Can we ever uncover the reason why some are healed while others languish? Such a question has haunted atheists and believers alike for centuries.

Yet even if Donahue was healed completely, events in October 2004 would have quickly derailed this alleged miracle for a very different reason: a lack of permanence. Life was going well for the youth. He was back at school, playing his guitar, and getting to know his friends and family again. It looked like things were finally getting back to normal for the Donahue clan. Then the phone rang. The results of a routine blood screening had some bad news. He would have to go back on dialysis, and seek a kidney transplant immediately. Those two essential organs were starting to fail again - precipitously. A donor would have to be found as soon as possible. After much searching and anxiety, Donahue's sister, Holly, turned out to be the perfect match. Yet even with the transplant, this young man will be on medication for the rest of his life.

As we can see here, even with a promising case like that of Joseph Donahue, there are often insurmountable obstacles when it comes to the miracle requirement. Donahue was not fully healed, and once recovered, did not stay well - both examples of issues that lead to disqualification by the Vatican.

Let us not fail to point out though that Joseph Donahue is alive today. To many, that is miracle enough.

Beyond the finer points of the miracle requirement, there are a host of other challenges that Nelson Baker will need to overcome to achieve canonization, one of which is himself. Baker does not appear to fit the profile of candidates whom the Vatican seems to favor for sainthood. First of all, he is an American-born man. Why is that a problem? Well, only because the Vatican has never canonized an American born man in the entire history of the Catholic Church. (We should note that in 1977, John Neumann, bishop of Philadelphia, became the first male US citizen to be named a saint. However, Neumann was a European, born in Bohemia in 1811, and did not obtain citizenship until 1848.[83])

To make matters worse, the numbers may also be working against Baker. There are approximately 28 active canonization causes vying for attention in the United States alone.[84] These include some men who are better known than Father Baker, including 1950s television star Archbishop Fulton Sheen, and Cardinal Terrence Cooke, the Archbishop of New York City who died in 1983. However, one piece of fortune can be noted in the "race" to become the first American-born male saint. Of the 28 causes, only two men have so far reached the beatification stage, and neither of them (Father Juniper Serra and the controversial Father Damien de Veuster) were born in the United States.[85] It seems reasonable to assume that contenders for the distinction of being the first American-born male saint can count on receiving a level of scrutiny usually reserved for presidential candidates, or lab rats.

Certainly, Nelson Baker could hold up to such a test, right? Upon closer examination, that may not necessarily be the case. This brings us to the second potential roadblock for Father Baker. He is a known miracle worker. The Church has always had a love/hate relationship with these "mystics." Even today there is a palpable "distaste"[86] in the Vatican for "wonder workers," according to *Newsweek* religion reporter Kenneth Woodward. The reasons are complex and have to do with theology, suspicion, and even basic human jealousy.

Miracles cannot be denied. They are scattered all throughout the Bible. Even Christ Himself was a gifted miracle worker, as were His Apostles. Yet how are we to recognize their existence and role as a part of God's natural order, but guard against creating Earthly figures who can sometimes reach cult status? Also, how are the faithful to know what is a miracle, and what is magic? What supernatural feats have been achieved through the work of the Evil One, as a display of his occult powers? To be absolutely clear, I am not suggesting that Baker has reached cult status, nor that his power came from the Devil, both of which are absurd with even a basic understanding of his intense piety and humility. What I am saying though is that, in general, the Church has run across its share of frauds throughout the centuries who have spoiled the credibility of the true practitioners of the divine.

There is also perhaps the beginning of a trend in the Vatican to move away from miracle workers, priests, and nuns who presumably are hard to identify with. The theory is that the Catholics of the world need more lay people to look up to as models of the faith. For example, in the early 1990s, a formal effort was begun to open a cause for Pierre Toussaint, the layman and for-mer slave from Haiti who worked with orphans and the poor in the early 1800s.[87] He has since achieved the title of Venerable. A possible shift towards laypersons is admittedly quite new, and perhaps too fresh to draw conclusions from. However, such a development does not necessarily have to take away from causes for the religious. Perhaps in hindsight this era will be viewed as a time for broadening the definition of those usually consid-ered eligible for sainthood, not a change in direction that would leave out a certain group such as priests.

Before we move on to the advantages that Baker has in his corner, we have not yet run out of bad news. Advocacy is the final major aspect of this arduous process to examine. The canonization journey requires long hours, tireless devotion, and reams of patience, all of which were personified by the greatest advocate yet known to Father Baker's cause, the late Our Lady of Victory Pastor Robert C. Wurtz. His death on December 12, 2006, at age 74, left a gaping hole in the effort to promote the sainthood of his predecessor. The monsignor died of cardiac arrest on an early Tuesday morning at Mercy Hospital in Buffalo. Like Baker, he had endured his share of suffering, including double knee replacement, and chemical therapy for colon cancer.[88]

Despite his physical ailments, the OLV pastor spent two decades promot-ing canonization for Baker. He kept in constant contact with the Vatican through emails and phone calls, submitting perhaps 25 miraculous claims attributed to Baker's intercession.[89] Wurtz was there at the beginning of the journey in the late 1980s when the cause for Baker was initiated.

Robert C. Wurtz was born on February 29, 1932,[90] just over four years before the death of Nelson Baker. He grew up working alongside his father on a farm in East Aurora that later became the property of Christ the King Seminary, his future alma mater. As a teen, the young man chose to take the name "Nelson" as his confirmation name. Wurtz was a graduate of Canisius High School, and (like Father Baker) Canisius College. He was ordained on his virtual birthday, March 1, 1958, after finishing his degree at Christ the King. He later went on to work in different capacities for Holy Family Parish in Machias, Our Lady of Pompeii in Lancaster, and as a business manager (another Baker parallel) at the seminary.[91]

Wurtz began a 33-year stint at Our Lady of Victory in 1974 when he was named assistant to the general manager of OLV Homes of Charity. In 1975, he was appointed the executive director of Baker Hall. In 1994, he became the third successor to Father Baker when he was elevated to pastor. One unique aspect of Wurtz's time as pastor was that he assumed a level of responsibility that only Baker himself rivaled. In 1996, Wurtz was named president of the newly formed Baker Victory Services (BVS), a merger of Baker Hall, the Infant Home, and several "group homes." This was in addition to overseeing Our Lady of Victory Hospital, the Basilica, and a parish of over 2,300 families. BVS alone annually provides care for over 3,600 children and their families.[92]

Amidst all of this, the late OLV pastor stayed devoted and focused on Baker's cause. He began each day at his tomb in private reflection, telling The Buffalo News the year before his death that he felt "permeated"[93] by Baker's presence. Many promising causes have ended abruptly when no one was left to pick up the mantle for the next generation to keep the memory of a holy person alive. He will be missed.

Certainly Wurtz's successor at Our Lady of Victory, Pastor Paul Burkard, is ready to assume the mantel of advocate, but a long road lies ahead for him, as he takes on all of the same responsibilities Wurtz had. Monsignor Burkard made a pilgrimage to Rome in February 2008 to submit "medical evidence"[94] in support of Baker's cause, but predictably could obtain no assurances on a timetable for canonization.

While Baker's supporters wait for progress from the Vatican, they can rest assured that their venerable prelate has at least a few advantages that can offer some encouragement. One is that Baker was an enormously busy man. Like a human dynamo, Nelson Baker never stopped doing things. Whether it was entertaining his boys with music, balancing the parish books, or seeing to the construction of new buildings (like the Basilica while he was in his eighties), the OLV pastor was never short on new responsibilities. In other words, he had very little time for a pursuit that can often tie up a cause for centuries: writing. Holy men and women who spend large portions of their lives pontificating in print on religious matters, often never have a chance at sainthood. If even one viewpoint of a candidate is found to be inconsistent with Church teachings, that could doom the entire cause. At the very least, the process will grind to a virtual halt as every word and phrase is dissected for heresy.

In this area then, Baker would be considered an extremely safe choice. He stayed away from "theological speculation"[95] his entire life. To be clear, let us not assume that this highly educated, multi-talented Renaissance man was unable to do so. Given the time, he could have postulated in at least four different languages. Time constraints and a life of humility prevented any such efforts. He may have even considered such a practice self-indulgent (as he did with pleasure reading), an inefficient use of time better spent helping people.

Another advantage Baker has is his reputation as a miracle worker. Yes, we did say that this could work against him in the Vatican, but it certainly has helped him here in Western New York where it is a common practice to pray to Nelson Baker for his intercession. The two-miracle requirement for sainthood has often hurt candidates who do not have a reputation for working miracles during there lives, such as Cardinal Terrence Cooke. One of the most difficult challenges in Cooke's bid for sainthood is to get the people of New York City used to the idea of praying to him for a miracle, something they did not do during his life in the latter half of the 20th Century.[96] Baker certainly has no shortage of people praying to him, now the better part of a century after his death. With so many people praying, this raises the chances that one case might be legitimate, and will hold up to the scrutiny of the Congregation for the Causes of Saints. The trick is to find those willing to come forward. Many who believe that they are touched by the miraculous seek no notoriety, nor invasion of their privacy for a matter they consider to be between themselves and God.

Finally, the cause for Nelson Baker can also point to a phenomenon that few other candidates possess to the extent found in Western New York: unparalleled dedication to him. This perseverance is evident at the end of every mass at Our Lady of Victory when the entire congregation says a prayer for the canonization of Father Baker.

The depth of this devotion was never more clear to me than on Christmas Eve 2005. My book-signing for *The Mysteries of Father Baker* was going well. At least I thought it was. Out of the corner of my eye I spotted two young men heading straight for my table. The look on their faces was fixed and serious. I thought perhaps I had cut them off in the parking lot, or that Santa had sent two messengers to confirm that I had not made the cut that year. Both were clad in jeans with longish hair and tattoos. They looked like rock stars. As it turns out, they were. The taller one reached the table and began to slowly pull out something from inside his jacket. He produced the oddest item that he began to nudge toward me on the table.

"Would you sign this?" he asked in a melodic voice.

It was my book.

"I'd be happy to," I managed to exhale.

I quickly learned that they were both from Lackawanna and were lifelong devotees of Father Nelson Baker. Not only that, they were founding members of the local rock band, "Rick James' Dealer," named after that second most famous citizen of Lackawanna. The band was formed in 1996 with Mike Osborne on vocals, Rich Smith on drums, Steve Sunick on guitar, and his brother Matt on bass.[97] Although they assured me that their sound was more punk than funk, they had in their repertoire a rousing number that

*Rick James' Dealer on Halloween night 2006 at C2 in Lackawanna. Left to right: Steve Sunick on guitar, Mike Osborne on vocals, Rich Smith on drums, and Matt Sunick on bass.*

always brought the house down at every gig. The tune in question was unabashedly titled "Make Father Baker a Saint." Yes, that's correct. A local rock band has a song called "Make Father Baker a Saint." Now if we could only get the Vatican to listen to modern rock, Baker might be that much closer to beatification.

I relate the above story not only to promote the continued success of the local music scene, but also to convey two irrefutable facts about Father Baker that I have learned first-hand in recent years. First, his appeal cuts across all demographic groups, young and old, women and men. Second, that appeal has lasted down to the present day, and will likely continue forward through new generations of Western New Yorkers as people continue to ask for his help, and remember his legacy over 70 years after his death.

Perhaps that is the true appeal of this man. He brings us all together and offers us something that is often hard to come by in this region.

Hope.

# ENDNOTES

[1] The American Heritage Dictionary 2nd ed. (Boston: Houghton Mifflin Company, 1985), 287.

[2] "A Catholic Encyclopedic Dictionary and Biblical Reference Guide" in The New American Bible (Wichita, Kansas: Catholic Bible Publishers, 1991), 102.

[3] Personal communications with the author, March, April 2008. Sue Nowak can be reached at www.susannowak@live.com.

[4] The summary of Baker's life borrows from Floyd Anderson, Apostle of Charity: The Father Nelson Henry Baker Story (Lackawanna, New York: Our Lady of Victory Homes of Charity, 2002), 130. This book was originally printed in 1960 under the title Father Baker, reprinted as a limited edition in 1974 under the title The Incredible Story of Father Baker, and updated in 2002 under the title Apostle of Charity: The Father Nelson Baker Story.

[5] The New American Bible (Wichita, Kansas: Catholic Bible Publishers, 1991), 1265.

[6] "Late pope inspired nun now cured of Parkinson's," The Buffalo News 31 March 2007.

[7] Personal interview with the author, July 19, 2006.

[8] Kenneth l. Woodward, Making Saints: How the Catholic Church Determines Who Becomes A Saint, Who Doesn't, And Why (New York: Simon & Schuster, 1996), 160.

[9] Ibid., 173.

[10] Ibid., 184.

[11] Anderson, 33.

[12] Ibid., 34.

[13] "Power to Raise Millions Miracle of Priest's Life," Buffalo Evening News 30 July 1936.

[14] Hongying Yang, et al. "Nutrient-Sensitive Mitochondrial NAD+ Levels Dictate Cell Survival," Cell 130, no. 4 (2007).

[15] Information on "The Coma Miracle" courtesy of personal interview with the author, December 2006.

[16] Information on the "The Sacristy Miracle" courtesy of personal interviews with the author, July 2006, August 2008, and January 2009. To be clear, Anne requested the rose from Jesus, not Saint Theresa, for those familiar with the same request often made of that saint. Also, we should note that it will remain unclear why Wurtz moved the letters to the Baker museum.

[17] Ruth Rejnis, <u>The Everything Saints Book</u> (Avon, Massachusetts: Adams Media Corporation, 2001), 204.

[18] Information on "The Ghostly Miracle" in part courtesy of personal communication to the author, 29 May 2006.

[19] Information on "The Ghostly Miracle" in part courtesy of personal interviews with the author, July 2006.

[20] Information on "The Healing Vision" courtesy of personal interview with the author 30 July 2008. Father Baker's age in this apparition is interesting. Lawrence said that he appeared to be in his 70s or 80s. This would have been how old Baker was when he knew her mother.

[21] Anderson, 13.

[22] Rejnis, 159.

[23] Donald Attwater, <u>The Penguin Dictionary of Saints</u> (New York: Penguin Books, 1985), 281.

[24] Anderson, 6.

[25] Bruce Lansky, <u>100,000 + Baby Names</u> (New York: Meadowbrook Press, 2006), 603.

[26] Information on "The Name Miracle" courtesy of personal interview with the author, 27 April 2008.

[27] "Was firefighter's recovery a miracle?" <u>Niagara Gazette</u> 7 May 2005.

[28] "Religion, science mix in Herbert's story," <u>The Buffalo News</u> 11 May 2005.

[29] "Was firefighter's recovery a miracle?"

[30] "Firefighter who came out of stupor dies," <u>The Buffalo News</u> 21 February 2006.

[31] Ibid.

[32] Ibid.

[33] Ibid.

[34] "Was firefighter's recovery a miracle?" The current pastor of Our Lady of Victory, Father Paul Burkard, declined to comment on the Herbert case to me.

[35] <u>Catechism of the Catholic Church</u>, 2nd. ed. (Washington, D.C.: United States Catholic Conference, 2000), 888.

[36] "Was firefighter's recovery a miracle?"

[37] Information on Bealtaine courtesy of Celtic World website, Mason Winfield, and www.applewarrior.com

[38] Rich Blake, <u>The Day Donny Herbert Woke Up</u> (New York: Harmony Books, 2007), 25.

[39] Ibid., p. 122.

[40] Ibid., p. 238.

[41] Ibid., p. 125.

[42] Ibid., p. 243.

[43] Ibid., p. 235.

[44] Information on "The Trio Miracle" courtesy of personal interview with the author, 5 June 2008.

[45] www.webmd.com/a-to-z-guides/amyloidosis-11083. Section in parenthesis is the author's.

[46] Eldra Solomon, et al., Biology 4th ed. (New York: Harcourt Brace, 1996), 1027.

[47] www.webmd.com/a-to-z-guides/amyloidosis-11083.

[48] www.webmd.com/ibd-crohns-disease/crohns-disease/what-is-crohns-disease. Section in parenthesis is not the author's.

[49] www.webmd.com/a-to-z-guides/amyloidosis-11083.

[50] Information on "A Gift of Sanctuary" courtesy of personal interview with the author, 25 July 2008.

[51] Catechism of the Catholic Church, 2nd. ed. (Washington, D.C.: United States Catholic Conference, 2000), 353.

[52] Information on "The Peace Miracle" courtesy of personal interview with the author, 24 June 2008.

[53] Frank Severance, ed. Peace Episodes on the Niagara Frontier, Buffalo Historical Society Publications, Vol. 18 (Buffalo, New York: 1914), 173.

[54] Information on "The Miracle of the Sacred Ground" in part courtesy of personal interview with the author 2 July 2008.

[55] Information on "The Miracle of the Sacred Ground" in part courtesy of personal interview with the author, 24 June 2008.

[56] Information on "The Miracle of One" courtesy of personal interviews with the author, 13 July 2008, and 30 August 2008.

[57] www.webmd.com/stroke

[58] Information on "A Chance Encounter" courtesy of personal interviews with the author, August 2008.

[59] Personal communication to the author, 13 August 2008, by Sister Eileen Pinkel.

[60] http://children.webmd.com/tc/congenital-torticollis-topic-overview

[61] Ruth Rejnis, The Everything Saints Book (Avon, Massachusetts: Adams Media Corporation, 2001), 197.

[62] http://www. ssadb.qc.ca. This is the official website of the Basilica of St. Anne de Beaupre.

[63] For further information on Baker and bilocation see The Mysteries of Father Baker, page 25, and pages 94-95.

[64] Helen I. Sullivan, "The Ladies of Charity in Buffalo," Catholic Charities Report: Ladies of Charity September 1962 (Buffalo, New York: The Catholic Charities of Buffalo, N.Y., 1962), 6. The Ladies of Charity are still in existence in Western New York. For example, they operate a thrift shop on Broadway to provide low cost consumer goods to the poor.

[65] Information on "The Chapel Apparition" courtesy of personal interviews with the author, 23 July 2008, and 4 August 2008, 6 January 2009.

[66] Anderson, 93.

[67] Information on "Baker's Final Earthly Miracle?" courtesy of personal interview with the author, 24 June 2008. The O'Connor family is a good example of how so many families pray to Baker for many things, not just one. He is always turned to in times of need. For example, Mary Lou O'Connor believes that her daughter, Sheila, was strengthened by Baker in her battle with cancer.

[68] Anderson, 123.

[69] Ibid., 124.

[70] Ibid.

[71] Information on Gauchat collection obtained by personal interview with the author, 1 June 2008.

[72] Webster's New International Dictionary 2nd ed., (Springfield, Massachusetts: G & C Merriam and Company), 2047.

[73] Ibid., 1950.

[74] Anderson, 77.

[75] Ibid., 108.

[76] Ibid., 109.

[77] Ibid., 107.

[78] Information on Metz collection obtained by personal interview with the author, 8 June 2008.

[79] Webster's New International Dictionary 2nd ed., (Springfield, Massachusetts: G & C Merriam and Company), 1498.

[80] Anderson, 134.

[81] The general understanding of the process is taken from http://www.catholic-pages.com/saints/process.asp.

[82] Information on Joseph Donahue is from Mary Bailey, "A family struggles after a medical nightmare," The Sun 17 March 2005.

[83] 14. The World Book Encyclopedia, 1998 edition, s.v. "Neumann, Saint John Nepomucene."

[84] Brendan I. Koerner, "Saint Makers," U.S. News and World Report, 3 January 1999.

[85] Ibid.

[86] Woodward, 158.

[87] Rejnis, 214.

[88] "Father Baker's 'champion' dies," The Buffalo News 13 December 2006.

[89] "Msgr. Wurtz helped pave the way for the sainthood of Father Baker," Western New York Catholic January 2007.

[90] "Msgr. Robert Wurtz followed in the footsteps of Father Baker," Western New York Catholic January 2007.

[91] "Father Baker's 'champion' dies."

[92] "Msgr. Wurtz is remembered as perfect choice to follow Father Baker," Western New York Catholic January 2007.

[93] "Father Baker's 'champion' dies."

[94] "Musical explores Father Baker's life," The Buffalo News 4 March 2008.

[95] "Saint Makers."

[96] Woodward, 22.

[97] Personal interview with the author, 29 May 2008.

# ABOUT THE AUTHOR

***John Koerner*** is the author of *The Mysteries of Father Baker* (Western New York Wares, 2005), *Supernatural Power* (Authorhouse, 2007, www.authorhouse.com/bookstore), and a co-author of *Haunted Rochester* (History Press, 2008). He has an MA in American History from the State University of New York, College at Brockport, where he was an award winning graduate student writer. Koerner graduated summa cum laude from the Honors Program with a BA in Communication/Journalism from St. John Fisher College in Rochester, New York. He is also a graduate of Saint Francis High School. His writing has appeared in the *Hamburg Sun*, the *Springville Journal*, and the *Next Step Magazine*. Born in Buffalo, Koerner is also an accomplished historical tour guide. He has worked as an instructional guide for Rochester's Neighborhood of the Arts, Roam Buffalo, and as a founding member of Haunted History Ghost Walks. Koerner is also a founding member and contributor to the Spirit Way Project (www.spiritway-project.com). Together with his wife, Tammy, he was also the co-director, and co-founder of Buffalo Literary Walking Tours. Koerner is a Social Sciences professor at Niagara County Community College, Genesee Community College, and Erie Community College.

# BIRTH OF A PUBLISHING COMPANY

The Buffalo area's most innovative publishing company hit two benchmarks in 2009 that few regional publishing houses attain. As the company observed its 25th anniversary, it also achieved the distinction of moving more than 270,000 books and other regional products into homes, schools and libraries since its inception.

Think of it this way. If we laid all the books we've distributed cover-to-cover in a paper path starting at the foot of Main Street near HSBC Center, the trail would stretch beyond the UB South Campus, snake through Williamsville, pass Batavia and end about 15 miles outside of downtown Rochester. Putting it a different way, we've distributed about 35 million pages of information about our region. We could hand out individual pages to every man, woman and child in New York State and Pennsylvania!

A pretty impressive path for a company that sprouted its roots in trivial turf.

The year was 1984 and the trivia craze was taking the nation by storm. As Buffalo journalist Brian Meyer played a popular trivia game with friends in his North Buffalo living room, he envisioned a game that tests players' knowledge about people and events in their hometown. Western New York Trivia Quotient sold out its first edition in six weeks and established Meyer as an up-and-coming young entrepreneur.

A year later, he compiled a book of quotations that chronicled the feisty reign of Mayor Jimmy Griffin. Meyer refuses to disclose how many six-packs were consumed while sifting through hundreds of "Griffinisms."

Meyer, a City Hall reporter for the Buffalo News, spent 15 years at WBEN Radio where he was a managing editor. As founder and president of Western New York Wares Inc., Meyer has collaborated with dozens of authors, artists and photographers. By 2009, the region's premier publisher of local books had been involved in publishing, marketing or distributing more than 150 regional products.

The Buffalo native is a graduate of the Marquette University, St. Joseph's Collegiate Institute and Buffalo Public School #56. He has taught communications courses at Buffalo State College and Medaille College. Meyer is treasurer of the Greater Buffalo Society of Professional Journalists' Scholarship Fund.

Meyer is assisted by Michele Ratzel, the company's business manager, and Tom Connolly, manager of marketing and distribution. The trio has 60 years of cumulative experience in regional publishing. Ratzel is an administrative assistant at Daemen College. Connolly works as a news anchor and producer at WBEN Radio. He co-authored *Hometown Heroes: Western New Yorkers in Desert Storm.*

# OTHER REGIONAL BOOKS

*Visit our Web site at www.buffalobooks.com for a complete list of titles distributed by Western New York Wares Inc.*

### The Mysteries of Father Baker
Healing the blind and deaf. Commanding the weather. Discovering a "Miracle Well." These are just some of the wonders that have been attributed to the intercession of Father Nelson Baker during his life – and even after his death. John Koerner examines the historical record surrounding these wonders and other signs worked by this devoted priest, renowned humanitarian and candidate for sainthood. The book includes dozens of vintage photos.
*ISBN: 1-879201-49-6*                                          *$12.95*

### Joe's Story: The Quietly Courageous Life and Violent Death of an Inner City Priest
Irony is a word that is overused. But what else do you call the death by slaughter of a man committed to non-violence who spent his life trying to alleviate the plight of those who killed him? Joe Bissonette reached adulthood convinced that his highest calling was to help and advocate for those with the least. The path appeared to be through the priesthood. In a book penned by his brother, Ray Bissonnette, readers are provided evidence of his success – even from the reflections of one of the priest's killers.
*ISBN: 1-932583-16-5*                                          *$15.95*

### Chicken Wing Wisdom: Western New York Stories of Life and Food Shared Around the Table
This book showcases local women and how their connection with food has impacted their lives, their communities and even the world. Christina M. Abt has penned a collection of stories about 14 Western New York women and their wisdom as it relates to food and nourishment. The tales cover a range of topics, from the creation and cooking of food, to teaching and counseling on the subject. The book also includes favored recipes contributed by each of the women profiled.
*ISBN: 1-879201-52-6*                                          *$13.95*

### Buffalo Soul Lifters: A Homespun Collection of Inspirational Stories
What is it about Western New Yorkers that sets us apart from everyone else? Is it our iron will? Our inner resolve? Our unbending spirit? This book showcases local people who have achieved stunning accomplishments by believing in themselves and in others. Some tales might be viewed as miracles. Others may be viewed merely as good deeds. But all will touch your heart. From Hunter Kelly and Father Baker, to the young boy who survived a plunge over Niagara Falls, and the plastic surgeon who treks to impoverished countries to help disfigured kids, all the folks in this book share a common trait. They remind us that hope is our lifeblood.
*ISBN: 1-879201-48-8*                                          *$12.95*

*Western New York 101: The 101 Greatest Moments in Buffalo History*
From Father Baker's quest to build a shrine that would stand among the most beautiful in the country, to the Pan-American Exposition and the Erie Canal's opening, the region has been a home to history. Dan Murphy pinpoints 101 banner moments, supplementing his informative text with vintage photos.
*ISBN: 978-1-879201-57-6*                                                      *$14.95*

*Remembering Old Buffalo: The Glory Years in Western New York*
Remembering is fun, especially when we recall all the fun we had in the "good old days." This book focuses on yesterday's fun: Crystal Beach, the Canadiana, Sunday rides in the country and holidays that created delightful memories. The late Joseph H. Radder's entertaining stroll down memory lane also showcases fun foods and many of the memorable local characters who made our lives so special. And let's not forget about yesterday's entertainment: radio, stage shows, the early days of television – even the Palace Burlesk.
*ISBN:  978-1-879201-59-0*                                                     *$13.95*

*Buffalo Voices & Visions: A Literary Journey & Paean to a Great Lakes City*
This book-length pastiche of poems, narratives, historical notes, fascinating "factoids" and vintage photos presents a unique tribute to Buffalo and its environs.

The late G.E. Murray engages both historical and contemporary voices, visions, insinuations, innuendoes and peccadilloes – all involving special moments that are unique to the times and spaces in Buffalo.

Western New Yorkers will find this literary journey across the region's rich landscape both entertaining and enlightening.
*ISBN:  978-1-879201-60-6*                                                     *$13.95*

*Village Ghosts of Western New York – Book One: Actors in the Half-Light*
Famous haunters, ghostly forms and wars in the heavens. Mason Winfield pays tribute to the hidden spiritual legacy of the region, including Underground Railroad mistresses and Seneca witches.
*ISBN: 1-879201-55-0*                                                          *$13.95*

*Shadows of the Western Door: Haunted Sites and Ancient Mysteries of Upstate New York*
A supernatural safari across Western New York. Guided by the insights of modern research, author Mason Winfield pens a colorful, provocative and electrifying study of the paranormal.
*ISBN: 1-829201-22-4*                                                          *$14.95*

*The Phantom Tour DVD: The 13 Most Haunted Places in WNY*
Full Circle Studios presents a 90-minute DVD experience that sweeps viewers away to places where events stay shrouded in silence. Mason Winfield serves as tour guide, while Jennifer Mucha hosts this riveting visual experience.
*ISBN: 1-879201-47-X*                                      *DVD  $19.95*

### Western New York Wild: Celebrating Our Rich Natural Heritage

More than 130 color photographs showcase dozens of natural wonders. David Lawrence Reade includes a "Wild Guide" that helps readers explore fascinating spots.
*ISBN: 978-1-879201-58-3*                                              *$19.95*

### The Four Seasons of Letchworth

A celebration of the nature and beauty of New York's Letchworth State Park as expressed through the exquisite images and reverent prose of David Lawrence Reade. The book includes more than 100 full-color photographs.
*ISBN: 878-879201-56-9*                                              *$24.95*

### Buffalo Snow

A full-color, beautifully illustrated children's book that tells the dramatic tale of a girl and her older brother stranded in a Buffalo whiteout. Written by Elizabeth Leader and Eve Tulbert, it's an inspiring story of how local residents open their homes and hearts to others.
*ISBN: 978-1-4243-2471-2*                                              *$6.95*

### Nine Nine Eight: The Glory Days of Buffalo Shopping

Author Michael F. Rizzo presents a fresh history of retailing in Buffalo. Rekindle your memories of an era when Buffalo's major streets were lined with stores. More than 100 photographs, ads and logos are woven into a lively text.
*ISBN: 978-1-4303-1386-1*                                              *$16.95*

### Crystal Beach: The Good Old Days

An American dream came true as U.S. entrepreneurs turned a wilderness lakeshore into the Crystal Beach amusement park. Erno Rossi's informative text is supplemented by more than 100 photographs.
*ISBN: 0-920926-04-5*                                              *$24.95*

### Victorian Buffalo: Images From the Buffalo and Erie County Public Library

Visit Buffalo as it looked in the 19th century through steel engravings, woodcuts, lithography and other forms of nonphotographic art. Author Cynthia VanNess has selected scenes that showcase everyday life and views of historic structures created by luminaries like Frank Lloyd Wright, Louis Sullivan and E.B. Green.
*ISBN: 1-879201-30-5*                                              *$13.95*

### The Erie Canal: The Ditch That Opened a Nation

Despite its shallow depths, the waters of the Erie carry an amazing history legacy. It was in canal towns like Lockport and Tonawanda where the doors to the American frontier were unlocked. Written by Daniel T. Murphy, the book includes dozens of photos.
*ISBN: 1-879201-34-8*                                              *$9.95*

*National Landmarks of Western New York: Famous People and Historic Places*
Gracious mansions and thundering waterfalls. Battleships and nostalgic fireboats.
Power plants and Indian long houses. Author Jan Sheridan researched nearly 30
National Historic Landmarks in the Buffalo-Niagara and Finger Lakes regions.
Dozens of photographs, maps and an index.
*ISBN: 1-879201-36-4*                                                 *$9.95*

*White Death: Blizzard of '77*
This 356-page softcover book chronicles one of the region's most dramatic historical
events. Written by Erno Rossi, the book includes more than 60 photographs.
*ISBN: 0-920926-03-7*                                                 *$24.95*

*Great Lake Effects: Buffalo Beyond Winter and Wings*
A unique cookbook that is filled with intriguing historical facts about the region.
The hardcover book has been compiled by the Junior League of Buffalo.
*ISBN: 1-879201-18-1*                                                 *$19.95*

*Buffalo Treasures: A Downtown Walking Guide*
Readers are led on a fascinating tour of 25 major buildings and a driving tour of
homes created by Frank Lloyd Wright. A user-friendly map and dozens of illustra-
tions by Kenneth Sheridan supplement an enlightening text by Jan Sheridan.
*ISBN: 1-879201-15-1*                                                 *$6.95*

*Church Tales of the Niagara Frontier: Legends, History & Architecture*
This first-of-a-kind book traces the rich history and folklore of the region through
accounts of 60 area churches and places of worship. Written by the late Austin M. Fox
and illustrated by the late Lawrence McIntyre.
*ISBN : 1-879201-13-5*                                                *$14.95*

*Symbol & Show: The Pan-American Exposition of 1901*
A riveting look at perhaps the greatest event in Buffalo's history. Written by the
late Austin M. Fox and illustrated by the late Lawrence McIntyre, this book offers a
lively assessment of the Exposition, bringing to light many half-forgotten facts.
*ISBN: 1-879201-33-X*                                                 *$15.95*

*Frank Lloyd Wright's Darwin D. Martin House: Rescue of a Landmark*
The untold story of the abandonment and rescue of the region's most architecturally-
significant home is recounted in vivid detail by  Marjorie L. Quinlan. The book
includes color photos and detailed architectural plans.
*ISBN: 1-879201-32-1*                                                 *$13.95*

*Buffalo's Brush With the Arts: From Huck Finn to Murphy Brown*
A fascinating adventure behind the manuscripts and million-dollar book deals,
highlighting the Niagara Frontier's connection to many creative geniuses.
Authored by Joe Marren, the book contains more than 20 photographs from
the Courier-Express Collection.
*ISBN: 1-879201-24-0*                                                 *$7.95*

## Shipping/Handling Charge:

Please include 8.75% sales tax for all orders in New York State and the following amount for shipping:

Orders up to $25....$4.00 (*shipping*)
    up to $50....$5.00
    up to $75....$6.00
    up to $100...$7.00
    over $100...$8.00

*Visit our Web site at: www.buffalobooks.com or write for a catalog:*

Western New York Wares Inc.
P.O. Box 733
Ellicott Station
Buffalo, New York 14205